E

"In 'Flourishing After Adversity - A 3-Step Action Plan to Transform Pain into Purpose and Embrace Joy Again', Laura Mangum Broome defines living proof of resilience. Her candid account and transformative journey truly inspires, laying out a practical road map to bouncing back stronger after life's hardest punches. She teaches readers how to go from surviving to thriving, using her faith, humor, and adaptive spirit as a guide. This book is a beacon of hope for anyone facing adversity and is a testament to human determination and love."

—Jonathan Milligan,
Author of Your Message Matters

"Laura Mangum Broome's 'Flourishing After Adversity' is more than a book; it's a lifeline. It courageously navigates the rough waters of life's unexpected challenges with clarity and compassion. As an embodiment of these qualities, Laura offers practical suggestions that empower readers to tap into their resilience. Her life journey and the inspiring case studies illuminate the immense strength and potential of the human spirit. 'Flourishing After Adversity' provides the perspective necessary to change what's in our control, enabling us to move beyond adversity and thrive."

—Marisa Shadrick,
Online Marketing Consultant & Certified Copywriter

FLOURISHING AFTER ADVERSITY

A 3-Step Action Plan to Transform Pain into Purpose and Embrace Joy Again

Laura Mangum Broome

AUTHOR ACADEMY elite

Library of Congress Control Number: 2023915222

Paperback: 979-8-88583-257-1

Ebook: 979-8-88583-258-8

To my family, whom I love to laugh with
and celebrate life together.

"Real optimism is aware of problems but recognizes the solutions, knows about difficulties but believes they can be overcome, sees the negatives but accentuates the positives, is exposed to the worst but expects the best, has reason to complain but chooses to smile,"
—**William Arthur Ward**

TABLE OF CONTENTS

BONUS: LIVE A LIFE WITHOUT REGRETS

INTRODUCTION

WHAT DOESN'T KILL YOU MAKES YOU STRONGER

So do not fear, for I am with you; do not be dismayed, for I am your God. I will strengthen you and help you; I will uphold you with my righteous right hand.—Isaiah 41:10 (NIV)

"Your daughter is in a coma."

Not the words you want to hear as parents when your 8-year-old daughter goes into the hospital for the third time for a routine operation to insert tubes in her ears. I was that daughter.

"There's a very slim chance she will come out of the coma," the doctor told my parents. "If she does, she most likely will have severe brain damage resulting from the high fever."

I'd had an adverse reaction to the general anesthesia they gave me. I had no such reaction from my previous two ear operations. This time my temperature rose to 107 degrees and my muscles contracted. The surgery team reacted quickly by icing down my body and giving me a muscle relaxant.

Unfortunately, I had an adverse reaction to the muscle relaxant, which caused my temperature to rise even higher. That's when I slipped into a coma.

I had experienced a malignant hyperthermia episode.

Malignant hyperthermia (MH) is a severe reaction to certain drugs used for anesthesia. This extreme reaction regularly includes a dangerously high body temperature, rigid muscles or spasms, a rapid heart rate, and other symptoms. Without immediate treatment, the complications caused by malignant hyperthermia can be fatal.

The higher the absolute maximum temperature and the longer the duration of anesthesia, the greater the mortality rate. At the time of my episode in 1970, the MH mortality rate was around 60-70%. After the introduction of the antidote Dantrolene in 1975, and further diagnostic testing, the mortality rate is now estimated to be less than 5%.

The only thing I remember from being in a coma was hearing my parents frantically talk to me in my hospital bed. I could hear them, but I couldn't open my eyes or move my fingers to respond to them. I felt like I was lying inside a dark box that prevented me from moving my body. I wanted to let them know I could hear them and that I felt fine. I couldn't understand why they were crying and talking to me as if I couldn't hear them.

Twenty-four hours later, an amazing thing happened: I awoke from the coma. My parents were elated when they heard the good news. The doctors confirmed I did not have brain damage, but my arm and leg muscles were so rigid that I needed physical therapy to straighten them. They also informed my parents I had a hole in my eardrum about the size of a quarter that could not be surgically corrected, resulting in a high percentage of hearing loss.

What a rollercoaster of emotions my parents experienced in 48 hours!

* * *

I wondered how I was going to recover quickly so I could go home and play with my friends and siblings. I missed them. Then my physical therapist walked into my room and introduced himself to my parents and me. *Well, this changes things*, I thought. Maybe I wasn't in such a hurry to recover after all.

Prince Charming, as I liked to call him, was tall, handsome, and had a smile that turned me into melted butter. He brought me an apple, or an orange, to my hospital room every day before our physical therapy sessions. At eight-years-old, a simple piece of fruit could buy my love and devotion to work hard on my straightening exercises. My mother said my face would light up as soon as he walked into my room, and the smile would not leave my face until an hour after he left.

He worked with me daily to straighten my arms and legs so I could walk on my own. It broke my heart to say farewell to my beloved Prince Charming when I was released from the hospital. I quickly recovered from my broken heart once I arrived home, greeted by family and friends.

* * *

My parents and I spent the rest of the year attending follow-up visits to my Ear, Nose, and Throat (ENT) doctor and more physical therapy appointments. Oh, how I despised my ENT visits because the elevator ride to the office caused my "bad" ear to pop uncomfortably.

My mother discovered she could coax me more easily to get on the elevator by pointing to the candy in the gift shop across from the elevator and bribing me with a Reece's Peanut Butter Cup after my doctor's visit. I was the better negotiator, however, and held out for two Reece's Peanut Butter Cups—one for going up in the elevator and one for going down.

Once my arm and leg muscles straightened out with physical therapy, I was running around and playing with my friends as if nothing had happened. I learned to wear an ear plug to protect the hole in my eardrum whenever I swam at our neighborhood pool or took a shower. The MH episode became "something that had happened to me" but didn't hold me back. I adapted to my new lifestyle and moved on with life.

Even though I have a 70% hearing loss in my left ear, I hear well overall and choose not to wear a hearing aid. I only have an issue when someone whispers in my "bad" ear or speaks quietly behind me. Other than wearing a medic alert bracelet, which the kids at school called *my dog tag*, my life was like the other kids.

* * *

I'm thankful I grew up in a family that has a sense of humor. We like to joke around and tease each other. We still chuckle about my "brain damage" and how they need to talk in my "good" ear when I need to pay attention to what they are saying. Humor is a good way to make light of a difficult situation…over time, of course. Laughter is a wonderful stress reducer because it releases endorphins that help you relax both physically and emotionally.

Through the years, and my many challenges, I learned better ways to handle trials and setbacks. Along the way, I became stronger in my Christian faith. God made me to fulfill his purpose for me on earth. Not what I thought my purpose was or even what my parents thought my purpose was. *God's purpose for me.*

When I follow God's calling, I find purpose and meaning which result in a fulfilling life. The Bible says we will always have trouble in this world, but we can put our trust in our Lord Jesus Christ, who overcame death on a cross and paid the debt for our sins. If he can overcome death, he can certainly help us overcome any type of adversity.

I can say without a doubt that God was with me during my many setbacks. He provided for my every need and helped me experience joy again. He is the living God, and He is with me always.

* * *

It was through overcoming my personal hardships that I developed the *iCope2Hope Resilience Framework*. This framework empowers individuals who struggle to move on after adversity to transform pain into purpose and flourish in life. You will learn action steps to conquer change, unlock your hidden strengths, and rediscover joy.

In the pages ahead, you will learn about a few of my trials and tribulations and how I overcame them. It wasn't quick or easy, but I persevered by taking baby steps each day and discovering that:

- I always have choices and I CAN focus on what's in my control to change.
- I don't have to like what I'm going through, but the sooner I CAN accept it, the sooner I CAN move on with my life and find opportunities to grow.

- I have untapped strengths inside me that I CAN access to reach my full potential.
- I CAN count my blessings throughout each day. Being grateful for even the littlest things changes my perspective.
- I CAN always find at least one good thing in a bad situation, even if it is the fact that my situation could be much worse, but it's not.

Two little words empowered me to regain control of my life: I CAN.

If you have experienced a major life-changing event, such as employment loss, financial loss, loss of a loved one, loss of relationships, or health loss, then this book will help you regain control of your life. How? By teaching you a process to develop a growth mindset, discover your superpowers, improve problem-solving skills, and live a life with no regrets.

(Note: If you are experiencing a difficult time moving through the grieving process to acceptance, I highly recommend you talk to a licensed therapist to help you deal with the different stages of grief: denial, anger, bargaining, depression, and acceptance. I benefited tremendously from counseling as I went through a recent life-changing event you will read about in Chapter 7.)

Life isn't fair. Change is constant. With resilience and hope, you can bounce back from setbacks and uncover the gift in adversity to find new meaning and purpose in life.

May the God of hope fill you with all joy and peace as you trust in him, so that you may overflow with hope by the power of the Holy Spirit. Romans 15:13 (NIV)

OVERVIEW OF THE ICOPE2HOPE RESILIENCE PROCESS

God allows us to experience the low points of life to teach us lessons that we could learn no other way.—C. S. Lewis

Adversity can make you bitter or better.

Adversity includes any major life event that disrupts your life, such as losing a loved one, loss of employment, loss of a significant relationship, loss of health, and financial loss. Adversity's disruption in your life can turn you into a victim or a survivor. The choice is yours.

A victim sees their situation as out of their control, unfair, and hopeless. They feel it's not their fault, someone or something is to blame. The victim may wait to be rescued. Over time, they become defeated, feel helpless, and develop a pessimistic outlook on life.

A victor, or survivor, understands life isn't fair. They adapt and overcome their circumstances through choices. It may not be easy at first, but they've learned through past challenges how to use their strengths and the resources to persevere and overcome setbacks along the way. They use creative problem solving to uncover opportunities to improve their outcome. Victors are flexible, resourceful, and have a positive outlook on life.

AFTER THE GRIEVING PROCESS

You may be familiar with the five stages of grief developed by psychiatrist Elisabeth Kübler-Ross in the late 60s: *denial, anger, bargaining, depression,* and *acceptance*. Everyone experiences grief in different ways and in different timeframes. There is no right or wrong way to grieve. These five stages of grief are not a step-by-step process, but a tool to help you identify the emotions going on in your heart and your head.

No matter how intense your loss is, there is life after grief if you acknowledge your emotions and work through them instead of trying to stop them. This process is called *constructive grieving*, which helps you move on to the acceptance stage. If you are having a difficult time moving on to acceptance, I highly recommend you contact a licensed therapist, and they can help you process your grief.

The iCope2Hope Resilience Framework best serves individuals who have accepted the necessary endings and are ready to move forward, but not sure where to start. You may feel overwhelmed and procrastinating about many pending decisions while fighting negative thoughts bouncing around in your mind. There is too much change happening at once for you to handle.

This framework gives you proven and practical action steps, resources, and tips that empower you to regain control of your life by conquering your thinking traps, bouncing back after setbacks, and uncovering opportunities to find new meaning and purpose in your life.

iCope2Hope Resilience Framework

Develop A Growth Mindset

FLOURISH

Uncover Opportunities

Overcome Challenges

THE ICOPE2HOPE 3-STEP RESILIENCE FRAMEWORK

In the Venn diagram above, developing a growth mindset will be the foundation for overcoming challenges and uncovering opportunities. The solid arrows represent this process.

As you manage your thinking traps and gain confidence to step out of your comfort zone to pursue new opportunities, you will be faced with setbacks which are represented by the dotted arrows. Instead of retreating to your comfort zone, you will learn coping skills to strengthen your resilience and overcome these challenges.

At the end of each chapter, I encourage you to complete the "Put It in Action" exercises to help you understand and implement the concepts.

I have also provided a case study at the end of each step as an example of each pillar of the framework. These are just a few of the inspiring stories of ordinary people overcoming extraordinary hardships.

STEP 1: DEVELOP A GROWTH MINDSET TO CONQUER CHANGE

In Step 1, you will learn what radical acceptance is and how it empowers you to accept what is out of your control so you can change what's in your control. I will discuss the different stages of planned change and unexpected change as well as why developing a growth mindset, instead of a fixed mindset, is the key to conquering change.

No matter how hopeless you think your situation is, you'll learn that you always have three things in your control. Also, by learning your ABCDEs, you will control your thinking traps and implement a positive outlook. At the end of this section, you will read how Scott Hamilton overcame a childhood disease to become an Olympic Gold Medalist in Men's Ice Skating at age 25.

STEP 2: DISCOVER YOUR SUPERPOWERS TO OVERCOME CHALLENGES

Step 2 will help you strengthen your resilience muscles by learning what a survivor's personality looks like. You will identify your skills, talents, passions, and character strengths to help you overcome challenges. By learning the iCOPE 5-Step Problem Solving Method you'll be able to solve any type of problem.

The inspiring story at the end of this section is about WWII Prisoner of War Soldier Louis Zamperini and how he overcame being lost at sea in a raft with no food and water, only to be rescued by the enemy and tortured. His perseverance and resilience are amazing.

STEP 3: THINK OUTSIDE THE BOX TO UNCOVER OPPORTUNITIES

Step 3 teaches you how to feel your fear and still step out of your comfort zone to find opportunities. By using creative problem solving, you'll learn how to discover serendipity (happy accidents) and implement the third alternative (1st-my way, 2nd-your way vs 3rd-how can we work together) to uncover opportunities and reach your goals.

FLOURISH IN LIFE

Finally, the Bonus section discusses how to live a life with no regrets by enjoying your bucket list now, how not to retreat to your comfort zone when obstacles arise, and the importance of leaving a legacy of resilience for future generations.

EXERCISE: PUT IT IN ACTION

1. Describe a recent life-changing event you suffered and how the experience changed your life in good ways and bad.
2. Explain how you plan to use the iCope2Hope 3-Pillar Resilience Framework to transform your hardship into hope and uncover opportunities to flourish.
3. Which one of the three pillars are you most excited to learn and why?

STEP 1

DEVELOP A GROWTH MINDSET TO CONQUER CHANGE

RADICAL ACCEPTANCE:
THE KEY TO MOVING FORWARD

When you argue with reality, you lose, but only 100% of the time.
—Byron Katie

I always dreamed of having a big family of my own. I wanted to have lots of children so I could have lots of grandchildren.

My father was an only child and my mother had three siblings. Growing up with many cousins close in age was so much fun. We got together often since we all lived in the same area.

My mother had three children with two pregnancies. We teased her that she got a two-for-one special since my sister and I were identical twins. My sister was born one minute before me. Two and a half years later, our brother came along.

I didn't marry until age 30, almost ten years later than most of my friends. Our son Justin was born right before my 35th birthday. Since I wanted several children, my biological clock quickly turned into a ticking time-bomb.

Within a year, I found myself pregnant again and I was ecstatic. My belly popped out quickly, so I happily pulled out my maternity clothes. However, at the 8 to 10-week mark, my baby's heartbeat stopped. It devastated me; this wasn't supposed to happen.

I sobbed uncontrollably while boxing up my maternity clothes. Even though my doctor assured me I wasn't to blame, I couldn't help but wonder if I caused my miscarriage. I dreaded telling my family and friends the sad news.

Another year later, I discovered I was pregnant again. This time, I was cautiously optimistic. I was careful not to do anything too physical that would cause me to lose this baby. Again, my baby's heartbeat stopped around the 8 to 10-week mark. With tears running down my cheeks, I asked the doctor, "What did I do to cause this?" He reassured me I did nothing and patiently answered my questions until I was ready to leave.

I went home and emailed my family and friends my news because I didn't want to make the phone calls again. Six months later, I donated my maternity clothes to charity.

A year and a half later, I discovered I was pregnant once again. I didn't want to tell anyone this time until after the first trimester. I told myself I would not buy more maternity clothes. I prayed so hard to God, asking him to let this pregnancy be a healthy one and for me and the baby to go full term. Everything seemed to go well. My belly popped out so fast that I had to go buy new maternity clothes.

One week after my shopping spree, I felt something was wrong. I frantically called my doctor's office for an appointment. They fit me in the next day. The doctor confirmed my worst fear. At around ten weeks, there was no sign of my baby's heartbeat.

That following Sunday at church, our pastor gave such a powerful sermon. The living God that took care of the Israelites while they wandered 40 years in the desert is the same living God that takes care of us during our times of need. The Bible says that the Israelites had enough food and water each day, and their clothes and shoes did not wear out during those 40 years.

Our pastor explained that God always keeps His promise of taking care of His children. It may not be what we want, but God always provides what we need. There are many more stories in the Bible that tell of His grace and mercy. Our pastor ended his sermon stating that God can bring good out of every situation, no matter how hopeless it looks. I took that sermon as a challenge. God was going to have to prove to me he can bring good out of my miscarriages.

I continually asked God why He allowed me to get pregnant just to lose my precious babies. He knew how much I wanted to have children. I was almost 40 years old, and my window of opportunity was closing. I was very grateful to have my son Justin, who was a happy, healthy

5-year-old. I wasn't ready to accept the fact that I would not have any more children.

A few weeks later, I received a thoughtful gift from a dear friend. It was a beautiful ceramic picture of the Serenity Prayer. I felt like God sent me this special prayer to tell me everything was going to be okay.

THE ORIGIN OF THE SERENITY PRAYER

Most people are familiar with the Serenity Prayer and associate it with Alcoholics Anonymous or other recovery groups. However, the original prayer came from a pastor's sermon in a small Massachusetts town during World War II. Over time, it was shortened from the original prayer to the version we know today.

God grant me the serenity to accept the things I cannot change, the courage to change the things I can, and the wisdom to know the difference.

Written by theologian Reinhold Niebuhr, a first-generation German American, this prayer was a response to the darkest days of World War II, when Hitler's evil Nazi regime wreaked havoc and threatened civilization. One line of the original version is:

The victorious man in the day of crisis is the man who has the serenity to accept what he cannot help and the courage to change what must be altered.

Niebuhr captured the ethical dilemma of his fellow German anti-Nazi emigrants who found themselves free from persecution in the United States but powerless to intercede against Hitler.

THREE PARTS OF THE SERENITY PRAYER

The Serenity Prayer is the foundation of my iCope2Hope Resilience Process. Learning how to accept what is out of your control and to change what is in your control strengthens your resilience to overcome difficulties and keep moving forward.

Like palm trees during hurricanes, we can bend without breaking. Unlike traditional trees, palm trees are not made of wood. Some of the cells are malleable, and others can easily flex and then return to their original position.

Resilience, then, is the ability to bounce back after adversity. I will discuss resilience in more detail in Step 2 of this book.

The first part of the Serenity Prayer is "*God, grant me the serenity to accept the things I cannot change.*" This phrase can be broken down into two concepts.

1. *God, grant me the serenity*: serenity means calm, peace, quiet, restfulness, stillness, trust in God and tranquility. Serenity is the opposite of anxiousness and stress. Don't you want serenity during a crisis?
2. *To accept the things I cannot change*: Acceptance doesn't mean you have to approve of it or even like it. Acceptance means "it is what it is." If we don't have control over a situation, we must acknowledge it and move on.

The second part of the Serenity Prayer is "*the courage to change the things I can,*" which can also be broken down into two concepts.

1. *The courage*: the opposite of courage is fear. Fear is what you feel when you must step out of your comfort zone. Comfort equals familiarity or no risk. Even if you are miserable in your comfort zone, you are still miserable. Changing your circumstances can be scary, but it is necessary at times. That's when courage rises to the top to help you move forward.
2. *to change the things I can*: this means to change what is in your control. This is powerful. You have the power to change your circumstances. You'll learn in Step 2 how to discover your superpowers and use them in new ways to overcome obstacles.

The third part of the Serenity Prayer is "*and the wisdom to know the difference.*" If you have control to change your situation, then change it. If you do not have control to change your circumstance, then accept it, acknowledge it, and move on. Sometimes it's not that easy at first because it's not a switch you can flip on and off. That's where radical acceptance comes in.

RADICAL ACCEPTANCE

Radical acceptance is the ability to accept difficult situations outside of your control, especially those that cause you pain and loss.

Life is not fair. You will encounter at least one injustice during your lifetime. Maybe someone else got the job you desperately wanted or were more qualified for, or your significant other fell in love with someone else and wants to end your relationship. Maybe it's a health diagnosis—heart disease, cancer, or a chronic illness—that will disrupt your life. Or maybe it was an unforeseen pandemic that required you to quarantine at home for over a year and you haven't been able to recover from it.

You don't have to like injustice, but you must learn to accept it to prevent the pain from turning into long-term suffering. That acceptance will eventually come as you move through the grieving process. It is imperative that you process all your emotions so you can get to the acceptance stage. Again, you may find it helpful to talk to a therapist about your emotions. The sooner you can accept the injustice, the sooner you can put your energy into changing something that is within your control.

Radical acceptance is the ability to accept situations that are out of our control and prevent pain from turning into suffering.

Pain	Suffering
• inevitable	• optional
• felt in our body	• felt in our mind
• tied to an event	• results when we dwell on a painful event
• heals over time	
• leads to positive growth	• stuck in unhappiness and hopelessness

Transform hardship to hope and uncover opportunities to flourish in life!

Pain is like a wound that needs time to heal. If you don't take care of your hurt feelings, they can make you feel stuck and keep hurting you.

If you let this go on for too long, you might start feeling like everything is against you and lose hope.

Fortunately, you have a choice.

PRACTICING RADICAL ACCEPTANCE

Change is inevitable. Growth is optional.

We will all experience hardship in our lives, but we have the choice to let adversity make us bitter or better. Once you work through your emotions, you can look at logical options to move forward.

The following signs and thought patterns might help you decide if you are avoiding accepting your situation.

- It's not supposed to be this way.
- I don't understand what I did to deserve this.
- I can't get past what happened.
- I can't deal with this.
- People shouldn't act the way they do.
- I'm never going to get over this.
- I don't understand why this is happening now.

Whatever your reasons for the lack of acceptance, these feelings are normal. However, when you try not to accept pain, you also choose not to feel joy or happiness. Avoiding your emotions creates more problems in the long run, such as depression and anxiety.

Practicing radical acceptance is a skill that improves the more you practice it. Below are some suggestions to help you get started.

- Create coping statements to help you get through difficult times.
- Accept things as they are instead of how you want them to be.
- Remind yourself that you can't change reality, but you can change your reaction to it.
- Understand what is within your control and what is outside of your control.
- If you cannot solve a problem or change your perspective on it, the answer might be to radically accept it.

- See a licensed therapist if you are unable to move through difficult feelings on your own.
- Check the facts and reality of what you are thinking to see if they are true.
- Allow yourself to let go of the need to control situations.

The following are coping statements that can be used when you struggle to accept what is out of your control.

- I can only control the present moment.
- I may not like what happened, but the present moment is exactly what it is.
- What I'm going through right now is hard, but it is temporary.
- I can accept what happened and still end up happy.
- I will get through this no matter what.
- There is no point in fighting against the past.
- I can choose to make a new path, even if I feel bad.
- When I remain rational, I'm better able to make good choices and solve problems.

What happens when you can't bring yourself to accept something when you know you must? That's called ambivalence.

AMBIVALENCE-THE STRUGGLE IS REAL

Ambivalence is the coexistence of two opposing feelings with the uncertainty of deciding. In my story above, I wanted to have another baby before I was too old, but I didn't want to have a high-risk pregnancy, or worse, a fourth miscarriage. I was ambivalent about what to do. Not making a decision was *still* a decision. It's an excuse for avoiding action.

Several people asked if I had considered adopting. My initial reaction was that I didn't want to adopt a child and then have the biological parent change their mind and take their child back. That would break my heart. Adoption wasn't an option for me at the time because I still desired to give birth to a child of my own, but I didn't want to have another miscarriage.

Changing your life for the better cannot happen if you procrastinate. The benefits of making a change must outweigh your fear of stepping out of your comfort zone.

Once you move past the ambivalence stage and accept your circumstances, you can change what's in your control and experience growth.

POSITIVE GROWTH FROM ADVERSITY

The Posttraumatic Growth Workbook by Richard G. Tedeschi, PhD, and Brett A. Moore, PsyD, ABPP, outlines five general types of positive growth that result from adversity.

1. **Personal Strength:** The daily battle of dealing with adversity can lead you to develop internal strength and realize you can face extreme situations successfully. You can manage negative thoughts, solve problems, and make significant changes in your life. Developing resilience skills increases your confidence to face future adversity.

2. **Improved Relationships:** Accepting help during your hardship is important and brings you closer to others. By learning how kind and compassionate other people can be, your relationships become stronger and more intimate. Growth happens because you become stronger by being able to accept help.

3. **Appreciation of Life:** One of the most common lessons learned from experiencing loss is that life offers so much. You find a greater appreciation for what you have. Your priorities may have shifted because you have a greater understanding of what truly is important in life.

4. **New Paths and Possibilities:** A saying I heard long ago still applies to my life now: "Obstacles are steppingstones to new opportunities." Obstacles are not impassable. You find a way to climb over it, go under it, or go around if you want to find the opportunity that awaits. New paths may cause a sense of loss of old goals but discovering a new option in life can become important and useful.

5. **New Understanding of Life's Meaning and Purpose:** As you struggle to understand why this adversity happened, you may sense an increase in spiritual matters or religious beliefs with an understanding of how to live life well. Overcoming adversity may spark a desire to give hope to other people going through the same experience. Things in your life that used to be upsetting may seem trivial now. Adversity can make philosophers out of people and reveal their new purpose in life.

THE REST OF MY STORY

In 2006, we adopted a handsome young boy named Grigory, age 9, from St. Petersburg, Russia. He was three months older than our son, Justin. Actually, Grigory adopted us, and our family was complete. I'll talk more about this experience later in the book.

In 2014, a movie came out called *Heaven Is for Real,* based on a 2010 New York Times best-selling Christian book *Heaven Is for Real: A Little Boy's Astounding Story of His Trip to Heaven and Back*, written by Todd Burpo and Lynn Vincent. The book documents the story of a near-death experience by Burpo's three-year-old son, Colton.

In one very touching scene in the movie, Colton recounted a story to his mom of a young girl greeting him in Heaven. He tells how this little girl reveals to him that she is his sister who died in their mommy's tummy. He explains to his mother that the little girl said Jesus had adopted her, and she couldn't wait to meet her parents one day. She said she didn't have a name because her parents had not named her. Colton's mother was speechless. As Colton communicated this story again to his father, it became clear to his parents he was telling the truth. They had never told Colton about the miscarriage they suffered before conceiving him. They didn't give their baby a name because they didn't know the sex. How else could Colton know such details?

As I watched this scene with tears in my eyes, I immediately felt great joy knowing that I will see my three babies in Heaven when God calls me home. What hope this scene brings to parents and families who have experienced a miscarriage!

I had dreamed of having five children, and God *had* answered my prayer. I had Justin and Grigory living with me and I had my three babies in Heaven. God is so good!

* * *

In the next chapter, we will learn the secret to conquering change—both planned change and unexpected change.

EXERCISE: PUT IT IN ACTION

1. If you are currently going through a difficult situation or have recently been through one, how can you apply the three steps of the Serenity Prayer to your circumstance?
2. List the things you must accept right now that are out of your control.
3. List the things in your control to change. We'll create action steps in an upcoming chapter.
4. What part of your situation are you struggling to accept? Why? Would talking to a licensed therapist in your area help you?
5. How can you practice the Radical Acceptance coping statements in your situation?
6. Which positive growth experiences would you like to achieve? Why?

THE SECRET TO CONQUERING CHANGE

Change the changeable, accept the unchangeable, and remove yourself from the unacceptable.—Denis Waitley

I'm a proud native Texan, born and raised in Houston. I thought I'd live my whole life in the Houston area until one day in early 2000, my husband received a phone call that would bring a big change to our lives.

His military orders with the Army Reserve came through to teach military science at the University of Pittsburgh for the next three years. I was very excited for him but apprehensive about moving 1,500 miles away with our three-year-old son and my 15-year-old stepson. I would be losing my support system of family and friends, those I relied on when my husband was away since I worked a full-time job.

My face tried to show some excitement as we began our long drive to our new state. But, if you peeked behind our over-packed Suburban, you could see deep heel marks in the road from me being dragged all the way to Pittsburgh.

We found out the day before we left Houston that my husband would have two weeks to help us get settled in our new home before he left for two months of training with the other military science instructors.

I felt the anxiety set in. I'm going to a new city in a new state where I won't know anyone, and everything will be unfamiliar to me. *"What if I get lost running an errand?"* (This was before GPS.) *"Who would I call?"* My husband assured me during our drive that everything would be fine. My frantic thoughts told me otherwise.

We arrived in Pittsburgh as scheduled and pulled into the driveway to our cute, ranch-style rental house in a nice, quiet neighborhood with rolling hills. We went inside the empty house and looked around. It felt very warm and cozy. My husband caught my eye and smiled. "See, everything will be just fine."

I tried to give him the benefit of the doubt and reluctantly gave him a half smile and nodded my head. Then his cell phone rang. He answered it and the smile disappeared from his face. He walked outside into the front yard to finish the conversation. The call didn't last long.

My husband walked inside the house trying to put his smile back on, but he was doing a poor job of it. He looked down, cleared his throat, and quietly explained that it was the movers on the call. The delivery of all our household goods was delayed for another two weeks because of a scheduling glitch with the drivers.

He was leaving in two weeks for training! My face turned white, tears filled my eyes, and my lower lip quivered. He put his arm around me and said, "Relax, everything will be just fine." I think I hyperventilated, but I can't recall.

My husband acted fast. Since our sons were busy playing outside in the yard, my husband got me in the car as fast as he could and played tour guide of our small town just north of Pittsburgh. As we drove by a quaint, old bookstore, he turned to me while pointing to their sign and said, "Look! There's your sign: Bloom Where You Are Planted. You love that saying." Slumped in my seat with my arms crossed, I gave a quick glance at the sign, scowled, and grunted.

We found the local grocery store, cleaners, Wal-Mart, and a few other shopping places not too far from our neighborhood. Again, more grunts from the passenger seat since I was too busy catastrophizing my life in my head instead of paying attention to his tour of our quaint town.

My husband quickly pulled into the parking lot of a mom-and-pop hardware store that was going out of business. Cheerily, he said, "Let's go in and see if we can find a good deal on something."

"I'll sit here while you go look," I responded grumpily. "I don't feel like getting out."

He promised we could leave in five minutes after we stretched our legs a bit. I begrudgingly followed him into the store, walking as if my feet weighed 50 lbs. each. He went to the right as I walked straight ahead, arms still crossed, while muttering, "Five minutes only! Then I'm leaving!" I bet my husband was thinking to himself, "*Two weeks can't pass fast enough!*"

This is what happens when you try to prepare for change, but don't prepare for unexpected challenges along the way. In my mind, my expectations for this move were linear, a straight line from Point A (Houston) to Point B (Pittsburgh). I didn't account for any detours or obstacles along the way which disrupted my expectations but taught me a big lesson.

Unexpected Change vs Planned Change

Just like death and taxes, change is inevitable. You have the power to choose despair or choose growth when facing any change.

I wanted to see our move to Pittsburgh as a fun, new adventure… until I was faced with obstacles. I didn't plan on our household goods being delayed while my husband was away for two months.

Our move to a new state was a planned change that I prepared for. However, it was the unexpected change that caused disruption and added a lot of stress to my life.

Researchers found that people going through an unexpected change experience a predictable cycle of emotions. Most experience feelings like Elisabeth Kübler-Ross' five stages of grief or loss: denial, anger, bargaining, depression, and acceptance.

You do not have to experience all these emotions or even experience them in the same order. However, if you find yourself stuck in the depression stage longer than six months, I recommend you contact a licensed therapist to talk to.

FOUR STAGES OF UNEXPECTED CHANGE

When you understand and expect the emotions associated with disruptive change, it becomes much easier to cope with challenges.

The four stages of unexpected change are:

Stage 1: Shock, Denial–When introduced to unexpected change, your first response may be shock or denial as you react to the disruption of your status quo.

Stage 2: Anger, Fear–Once the reality of the disruption sinks in, you may fear the impact of it and/or feel angry, which results in actively protesting the unexpected change. If you resist change and remain at Stage 2, moving forward will be unsuccessful.

This is a very stressful and unpleasant state to be in. It is much healthier to move forward to Stage 3 where Stage 2's pessimism and resistance give way to the beginnings of optimism and acceptance.

Stage 3: Acceptance–This is where you stop focusing on what you have lost, or what's out of your control. You begin to let go and accept the disruptive change or necessary ending. You start to test and explore what this change means to you and how to adapt to the reality of what's good and what's not so good in your life.

Stage 4: Commitment–Now you are ready to embrace the change and rebuild your new reality. Only when you get to this stage can you reap the rewards of change. You are ready to move onto the next phase of your life.

When I tried to embrace moving to a new state, I built up excitement about all the positive things that would happen.

However, I didn't prepare myself for a few of the not-so-good things about our move, because I didn't know how to plan for disruptions. My oversight put me in Stages 1 and 2.

FIVE STAGES OF PLANNED CHANGE

Don Kelley and Daryl Conner developed their Emotional Cycle of Change model in the mid-1970s, and they outlined it in the *1979 Annual Handbook for Group Facilitators*.

Their Emotional Cycle of Change has five stages:

Stage 1: Naïve Enthusiasm—You may be excited to get started with a planned change, but you may not be aware of the difficulties you could face because you focused on *doing* instead of *thinking*. However, capitalize on your excitement and list all the benefits that you hope to achieve because they will motivate you later.

Stage 2: Apprehensive Cynicism—As your new situation advances, you may begin to feel negative emotions when obstacles arise. The more frustrated you become with your ability to handle these challenges, the more likely you are to quit altogether. This is the point at which you "check out" and move on to another new, exciting situation which takes you back to Stage 1.

If you feel like giving up when obstacles arise, revisit your goals to see if you need to break them down into smaller goals or adjust them to match your new knowledge of your situation. The more you acknowledge your doubts and fears and understand why you feel that way, the easier it becomes to push through your negative thoughts and move onto Stage 3.

Stage 3: Hopeful Reality—Once you've pushed past doubt, your cynicism or pessimism should start to wane. You may still feel apprehensive, but you're more likely to solve problems now that you are more familiar with your situation.

Stage 4: Confident Enthusiasm—In this stage, you start to feel confident that you made the right choice. You'll see the change as positive because you have more experience with it. You may begin to encourage and support others who are in an earlier stage of the change process. This is an effective way to strengthen your knowledge: mentoring someone through a similar change.

Stage 5: Achievement—You're probably feeling a lot of satisfaction at this stage because you've worked through the obstacles and made change a success. Celebrate your accomplishment! Now you have the confidence to manage your emotional responses when the next change comes about.

THE SECRET TO CONQUERING CHANGE

The secret to conquering change is developing a *growth mindset* from a *fixed mindset*.

A fixed mindset is when you put limits on your abilities to handle change. You tend to see yourself as either succeeding or failing. When things get tough, you either give up, lose interest, or move on to something easier. It's easier to stay in your comfort zone, which is safer, than to take a small risk and challenge yourself.

A growth mindset means you see your actions as either successful or needing improvement, never as failure. When you try something new and it doesn't go as planned, you see it as a teachable moment or a lesson learned, but you don't see it as a failure. Failure is when you stop trying. By having a growth mindset, you tell yourself, *"I haven't achieved it...yet."* The word *yet* implies you will find a way to reach success. By persevering, you develop resilience, which builds confidence in your abilities.

THE REST OF MY STORY

As my husband and I went our separate ways inside the small hardware store, I stewed in my grumpiness and wasn't even paying attention to my surroundings. Suddenly, I heard a woman's voice shout "Laura!" I looked up and stopped in my tracks. She was standing fifteen feet in front of me. "Martha!" I shouted back. We ran toward each other, squealed, and hugged, while people in the store stared at us as if we had gone crazy.

My husband quickly walked over to us, and I ecstatically introduced him. "Martha is a college friend of my childhood friend Jennifer, and we all hung out together when I'd go visit them on the weekends!" I looked back at Martha and laughed. "Jennifer told me you lived in Pittsburgh, but I assumed you lived on the other side of the city from us."

Martha replied, "My husband and I moved here two years ago, and we live ten minutes away from this store! Jennifer told me y'all were moving here, but I didn't know how to contact you. In fact, I had finished running my errands and was going home when I saw the 'Going Out of Business' sign. I stopped at the last minute to see if they had tomato plant cages. I've never noticed this store before until a few minutes ago."

We cheerfully exchanged phone numbers and addresses, and Martha said she'd be happy to help me with anything I needed while my husband was away.

As my husband and I walked out of the store, I beamed with joy and felt like I was walking on a cloud. I looked at him and said, "See, God has my back. What are the odds of me running into Martha unexpectedly like this? And Martha lives ten minutes away from us! Everything is going to be just fine now."

My husband smiled at me, rolled his eyes, and replied, "At least you can bloom where you are planted now."

My unexpected encounter with Martha kicked me out of *Stage 2: Apprehensive Cynicism* and pushed me into *Stage 3: Hopeful Reality*. I knew Martha was a fellow introvert and enjoyed staying in her comfort zone, so if she could move 1,500 miles away from home and adapt to a new environment, then I could, too.

And I did. While my husband was gone those two months, I enrolled my stepson into high school, found a wonderful daycare to enroll our three-year-old son in, unpacked our household goods which eventually arrived, and found myself a 30-hour a week part-time job. Funny thing, I became so busy taking care of things that were in my control that I didn't have time to contact Martha.

That 15-minute encounter gave me the confidence to try and do things on my own, knowing Martha was only a phone call away if I needed help. I did experience small setbacks along the way, but I resolved them on my own and continued to move forward. I had more growth that year than I can remember, and I grew confident in my problem-solving skills.

* * *

In the next chapter, you'll learn how to control thinking traps with three things that are always in your control, no matter how hopeless you feel about your situation.

Exercise: Put It in Action

1. Do you see change as a disruption or a gift? Why?
2. What changes are you experiencing in your life now?
3. How can you prevent "checking out" in Stage 2: Apprehensive Cynicism when obstacles arise?
4. Do you currently see yourself having a fixed mindset or a growth mindset? Why?
5. Make a list of changes you have conquered in your past and how you did it. Keep this list handy and refer to it the next time you fear change.

THREE THINGS ALWAYS
IN YOUR CONTROL

*Incredible change happens in your life when you decide to take control
of what you do have power over instead of craving control
over what you don't.—Steve Maraboli*

"What do you mean we can't contact Grigory?" I shouted frantically. "He's expecting us to complete his adoption soon. Without contact from us, he'll think we changed our mind. This is terrible, just terrible!" I panicked, pacing back and forth.

In the summer of 2005, we were part of a group of families who took part in our local adoption agency's two-week "American Summer Camp" where orphans arrived from St. Petersburg, Russia to interact with their potential adoption families. The children were under the care and supervision of the orphanage director, her assistant, and their Russian adoption liaison, who also acted as their English translator.

The happy interactions went well between the families and the children, ages six to ten. Grigory, age nine, stayed by my side almost the entire time while my son Justin, also nine, enjoyed playing games outside and making crafts inside with the rest of the children. Grigory placed his claim on me and would let no one "steal" his family from him.

After many meetings, home visits, and evaluations, we were approved to make our first official visit to St. Petersburg, Russia in late fall of 2005. We were very excited. Justin and I had never traveled outside of the United States, so we weren't sure what to expect. St. Petersburg is a beautiful city with a rich history.

Our visit to Grigory's orphanage went well, and he showed us his room where he shared with two other children. They each had their own bed and a drawer or two in the same dresser. The orphanage administrators kept us busy throughout the day with lots of fun activities.

There was one little girl, around the same age as Grigory and Justin, who followed us around the orphanage. Her precious smile melted my heart. I took a picture of her while she twirled around in her pretty dress. I whispered to my husband, "We will come back and adopt her next time." Actually, I wanted to adopt all the children who looked longingly for a family to belong to.

By early 2006, six out of the ten families in our group returned to St. Petersburg and completed their adoptions. We were so happy for them and eagerly awaited our turn.

We finally received a call from the adoption agency. The good news we expected to hear was not the reason for the call.

We were informed that our adoption process, along with three of the remaining families, was on hold. The Russian government issued an immediate six-month moratorium on all international adoptions and would decide whether to cancel any pending adoptions.

Our hearts sank. We didn't expect this major setback. Grigory needed to know that we still wanted him to be a part of our family.

Our adoption coordinator sadly informed us that the Russian government also cut off all communication between the adopting families and the orphanages. It devastated us. Six months of no contact would seem like a lifetime. What were we going to do?

FEELING OUT OF CONTROL

Change is especially hard to deal with when there are so many unknown variables. It makes it almost impossible to find options because there are too many to choose from. The thought gremlins come out and cause worry and anxiety and make you play their dreaded game of "What If".

- "What if I can't support myself after my divorce?"
- "What if the test results come back positive for cancer?"
- "What if I lose my house?"

- "What if I can't find a job that pays enough?"
- "What if _____?" (Your turn to fill in the blank.)

When we focus on what's out of our control, it's like sitting in a rocking chair and expecting to move across the room. No matter how hard you rock back and forth, you can't move forward.

Worrying about things you have no control over reaps the same consequence. You worry because you don't know what will happen because it's out of your control.

Unresolved worry turns into suffering, which turns into helplessness, which turns into hopelessness.

You can't change the unchangeable, but you can change what's in your control by taking action.

THREE THINGS ALWAYS IN YOUR CONTROL

No matter how bad your situation looks, there are always three things in your control:

1. Your thoughts.
2. Your words.
3. Your actions.

Did you notice there is a common word listed in all three? Yes, "your!" You are in control of yourself! You don't have control over other people's thoughts, words, and actions, but you have control over yours, and that is powerful.

YOUR THOUGHTS

You are in control of your thoughts. Your thoughts can lift you up or tear you down. Your mind is the control center for your body. Negative thoughts fill your body with negative feelings. Positive thoughts fill your body with positive feelings. It's your choice.

No one can control your thoughts but you. Isn't that empowering?

When you experience difficult times, it's normal for your mind to be engulfed in negative thoughts. But focusing on negative thoughts all the time causes you to catastrophize or spiral down into the depths of despair. We will discuss thinking traps later in this chapter.

One way to control negative thoughts when adversity hits is to acknowledge them and think, "Wait a minute. I can't do *that*, but I can do *this*." Then do it…or make a plan of action with baby steps and then do it. Baby steps work!

Sometimes "I can do this" means just doing what you can at that very moment. Getting out of bed and getting dressed is a great way to start the day. Make your bed so you don't crawl back into it. This works for me when I get in a discouraged mood. My bed looks so nice when it's made, especially with a couple of cute throw pillows. It's my first accomplishment of the day.

It's so easy to focus on what we can't do, but there are so many things we CAN do. So do one of them! Remember, you can do anything you put your mind to, even for 15 minutes. If 15 minutes seems too long at first, do it for two minutes. Sometimes just starting is the hardest thing to do. Most of the time, you'll continue after two minutes. If you don't want to continue, then don't. Try again a couple of hours later or the next day. Set a timer and try it.

Eight Common Thinking Traps to Avoid

Thinking traps are negative thoughts that are fueled by emotions instead of facts. They are based on your experiences in life and your beliefs.

In the book *The Resilience Factor: 7 Keys to Finding Your Inner Strengths and Overcoming Life's Hurdles*, Karen Reivich, PhD, and Andrew Shatte, PhD, discuss eight common thinking traps and how to avoid them.

1. **Jumping to conclusions**: This occurs when you quickly make a conclusion based on limited information or emotion. Avoid this by slowing down and evaluating the facts in front of you.
2. **Mind reading**: You assume you know what the other person or people are thinking, or vice versa, and act accordingly. Avoid this by speaking up and asking questions to clarify what

you understand to be the facts or confirming your and others' responsibilities.

3. **Personalizing**: You take sole responsibility for the blame. Avoid this by looking outward to acknowledge other people who are responsible or accountable for the situation as well.

4. **Externalizing**: You blame others and are not held accountable for your involvement in the matter. Avoid this by holding yourself accountable for your actions.

5. **Tunnel Vision**: You focus on one aspect of the problem. Avoid this by refocusing on the big picture instead.

6. **Overgeneralizing**: You use the words "always" and "everything." Avoid saying these words by being specific.

7. **Emotional reasoning**: You rely on emotions to make decisions. Avoid this by relying on the facts of the situation.

8. **Magnifying and minimizing**: You magnify the bad and minimize the good. Avoid overcompensating by finding a balance between the good and bad in your situation.

MY RESILIENCE BIBLE

In 2011, I attended a four-week U.S. Army Comprehensive Soldier Fitness - Family Resilience Academy at Fort Hood, Texas where I, and other local military spouses, learned how to become more resilient while our Soldiers were away at training or on deployments. Based on my personal experience, I also wanted to share this knowledge with military families of Army Reserve/National Guard Soldiers who didn't have access to resources like the families of the Army Soldiers on active duty.

The Family Resilience Academy is based on the U.S. Army Master Resilience Trainer (MRT) course, which provides face-to-face resilience training, and is one of the foundational pillars of the Comprehensive Soldier Fitness program. The 10-day MRT course is the foundation for training resilience skills to sergeants and for teaching sergeants how to teach these same skills to their Soldiers. Reivich and Martin E. P. Seligman, PhD, the father of Positive Psychology, developed this program with the Army.

Each participant in our class was given the book *The Resilience Factor*, and it became my resilience bible during the course. I still refer to it today because of its invaluable information. One exercise I learned was a game changer since I struggled to control my thinking traps. I hope it will be a game changer for you as well.

LEARNING YOUR ABCS AND DES

In *The Resilience Factor*, this exercise is called Learning Your ABCs. However, in Seligman's book *Learned Optimism: How to Change Your Mind and Your Life*, he refers to it as ABCDEs, which I prefer. You'll see why.

First, let's look at the ABCs.

- **Adversity:** Record your description of what happened, not your evaluation of it. Be objective about the situation and write down the facts.
- **Beliefs:** These are how you interpret the challenge based on your experiences and values throughout your life. Separate beliefs from feelings. (Feelings will go under "Consequences.") You can evaluate the accuracy of beliefs. They may or may not be based on facts.
- **Consequences:** Record as many feelings you have about the adversity and the actions you took.

Now, look for a link between your beliefs and consequences. Seligman states that pessimistic explanations will create passivity and dejection. Optimistic explanations energize addressing the challenge. If you change the regular beliefs that follow adversity, then your reaction to adversity will change at the same time.

Now, we'll add the DEs.

- **Dispute:** Go on the attack and give each negative thought an argument about why it is wrong. You become a detective by asking, "What is the evidence for this belief?"
- **Energize:** By disputing your beliefs, you can go from despair to hope and move forward with optimism.

THE ABCDE MODEL IN PRACTICE

Imagine I've called my adult son several times about a computer issue I'm having. I've left him several voicemails, but he hasn't returned my calls. I wasn't too concerned at first, but now it's been almost a week and I haven't received a call, text, or email from him. My frustration turns to worry. Is he ignoring me? Is he mad at me? Did something horrible happen to him? Why hasn't he called me back? What could I have said the last time we talked that upset him?

I recognize I'm spiraling down into despair. I tell myself to stop catastrophizing while I quickly grab my ABCDE notes I keep handy on my refrigerator.

I start the process.

- **Adversity:** My son hasn't contacted me for almost a week, and I need his help with a computer issue.
- **Belief:** I jump to a conclusion (thinking trap), "He used to call me back the same day. I'm not important to him anymore!"
- **Consequences:** I'm hurt, sad and become depressed the rest of the day. I feel insignificant because my son has ignored me.
- **Dispute the belief:** I reflect, "This type of thinking is ridiculous. I know my son loves me very much, and he is very attentive to me. There could be many reasons why he hasn't called me back. Maybe he's busy with his new job or he's busy with family activities. He'll call me back as soon as he can. He always does and apologizes for his delay."
- **Energize:** I keep busy by running errands in the morning and meet a friend for lunch. Later that evening I received a phone call from my son. He apologized for being swamped at his new job. Instead of making him feel guilty, I accept his apology and we have a pleasant conversation before he talks me through my computer issue. We both enjoy the conversation very much and make plans to meet for dinner with his family next week to try a new restaurant in town.

When you dispute your insecure belief, you keep from catastrophizing the situation. Looking at it from a logical point of view based on my son's normal behavior, I know he will return my call as soon as he can. Therefore, I can take care of things that are within my control such as running errands and meeting my friend for lunch.

YOUR WORDS

Your tongue has incredible power when it comes to speech. It can say words to lift people up, and it can say words to cut people down. That includes self-talk. Our thoughts control our words, so negative thoughts give birth to negative self-talk. Adversity can make you bitter or better. You can complain about your situation, or you can hunt for the good stuff and be grateful your situation is not worse.

When you are on the emotional rollercoaster of dealing with adversity, you can choose to get off the rollercoaster. Remember the statement we talked about earlier? "I can't do *that*, but I can do _____."

You can play a game with yourself called *How Many Positive Things Can I Say About One Negative Thought*. For every complaint you have about your situation, you must find at least two good things to be grateful for.

From my story above, I could say, "Even though I can't contact Grigory during the moratorium, I can think positive and plan Grigory's homecoming celebration, and Justin can help me."

It's okay to have a bad day, but it's not okay to have a bad week. It's alright to talk about your frustration, but don't keep focusing on it (pain vs. suffering). Take positive action.

YOUR ACTIONS

Your thoughts and words lead to your actions. Learn to get them in sync, and you will find opportunities to improve your situation.

In the past, when I became stressed or frustrated, I chose to comfort myself with food, but it actually did me more harm than good. Dealing with my emotions with food temporarily comforted me but caused me to gain weight, which made me feel worse in the long run. My actions of stress-eating didn't reduce my stress, it caused more stress.

Make a list of positive things you can do right at that moment that diffuse a frustrating or anxious situation. I'm talking about doing something positive AND productive.

- Take a 10–15-minute walk in nature and appreciate the beauty.
- Work on a hobby that brings satisfaction.
- Call a friend who makes you laugh or invite them to see a movie with you.
- Listen to your favorite music or an audiobook to keep your mind busy.
- Perform a small act of kindness for someone.
- Come up with other ideas that bring you joy.

Now that you have a list of positive activities you can do to feel better, do them. Don't *talk* about doing it, do it!

It's not beneficial to be left alone with your negative thoughts because you will ruminate, which is unproductive and results in feelings of anxiety, helplessness, and hopelessness.

No matter how bad your situation is, you can always find at least one good thing to focus on and talk about. Learn to seek out and find the good stuff because the good stuff brings hope and hope moves you forward.

THE REST OF MY STORY

I couldn't do anything about the Russian government's six-month moratorium, but I had hope because God got us this far in the adoption process. My son Justin and I worked on Grigory's room to get it ready for his homecoming. We knew Grigory had very few possessions in the orphanage and would be so excited to have his own bedroom and personal things. Justin and I had fun working on this exciting project.

Thankfully, there was so much opposition to the Russian moratorium from the United States and other countries that it ended after five months. Our adoption process was back on track! The four remaining families, including ours, eagerly picked up where we left off. Two families flew to

St. Petersburg to complete their adoptions and came home with their new family members. We were giddy with excitement because we were next.

Since we would be in Russia at the end of November and most of December, Justin stayed in Houston with my family while he completed his homeschool assignments. Everything went smoothly in Russia until we found out that a big snowstorm was headed our way, just as we were getting ready to go to court. We wanted to finalize the process quickly to avoid the snowstorm and get home in time for Christmas.

God was with us once again. With our son Grigory Broome, we left Russia the day before the big snowstorm hit and walked through our own front door just before midnight on Christmas Day, 2006. My stepson James and our son Justin greeted us and their new brother with big, happy hugs.

They let Grigory open his first Christmas present, which was a foosball table, since Grigory was a big soccer fan, or futbol fan. He couldn't wait to challenge one of his brothers to a game, despite the exhaustion of our long trip home.

Six days later, we celebrated Grigory's 10th birthday. I told him everyone was shooting off fireworks in honor of his first birthday in America. That Christmas became one of our most treasured memories.

God can bring good out of every situation, even in a six-month moratorium.

* * *

In Step 2 of the book, you will learn how to strengthen your resilience by discovering your superpowers to overcome challenges.

EXERCISE: PUT IT IN ACTION

1. Which thinking traps do you struggle with? What action steps can you take today to control your thinking traps?
2. When adversity hits and you feel your life is out of control, what specific actions can you take to implement the three things that are always in your control: your thoughts, your words, your actions?

3. Using the ABCDE Model, make a plan of action to dispute a belief you are struggling with:

- Adversity -
- Belief (thought) -
- Consequence (feeling) -
- Dispute the belief -
- Energize the situation -

CASE STUDY: SCOTT HAMILTON

FROM UNDIAGNOSED ILLNESS TO OLYMPIC GOLD MEDALIST

Everything that I've ever been able to accomplish in skating and in life has come out of adversity and perseverance.—Scott Hamilton

Scott Hamilton at the 1984 Olympics in Sarajevo where he won the gold medal in Men's Singles Ice Skating. Courtesy of figureskating.about.com

In his book *Finish First: Winning Changes Everything*, Scott Hamilton recounts growing up as a sickly child with an undiagnosed illness. At age four, he battled a rare illness that came with all kinds of unpleasant symptoms, one being stunted growth. Throughout school, the kids teased and bullied him because he was shorter and smaller than his classmates.

While Scott was young, his life was consumed with hospital visits and doctor appointments. By age 9, he and his parents became physically and emotionally spent. The family physician suggested they take a morning off once a week and do something fun.

His parents began taking Scott to the new ice-skating rink in town and eventually signed him up for ice-skating lessons. Like most beginners, Scott went around the rink holding onto the wall. What he and his parents discovered during his first few times ice-skating was that he breathed much better in the cold air. After a while, he was skating as well as the healthy kids were.

The cold, moist air helped with his lung condition and the constant movement on the ice rink helped Scott digest food properly. The more he focused on ice-skating, the more energy he had and the better he skated. Soon he started competing. He found out his stunted height of 5 ft 3 inches actually leveled the playing field on the ice rink.

Through consistent practice and dedication, Scott achieved his dream of winning the Gold Medal in the 1984 Olympics at the age of 26. Known for his famous backflip, Scott Hamilton is one of the greatest ice-skaters of all time.

Scott Hamilton doing his famous backflip.
Courtesy of pinterest.com

Since 1997, Scott has experienced testicular cancer and three brain tumors. His brain tumors were pituitary tumors recurring from the one he had when he was a young child, even though the symptoms went away. Looking back, Scott says without that undiagnosed brain tumor, he would have never gotten into ice-skating.

In Scott's June 6, 2020, blog in *Cure Today*, "*Make It Count: Scott Hamilton Discusses His Cancer Journey*", he writes, "So, here's what I want you to know about survivorship: It's obviously a true blessing and gift. Without the cause and reason to survive, our lives would look and feel a lot different, and probably not for the better."

Scott continues, "Maladies and struggles are unavoidable and, in many cases, the most important episodes of our lives. They shape us, empower us and allow us to be the people we cannot be without them.

But mostly, they give us a second chance at life. It's what we do with that second chance that truly defines us. Make it count!"

When Scott talks about finishing first, it's not just about beating your competitors. Finishing first means understanding your life's purpose and putting your whole heart into being the best at what you do. Break through your perceived limitations, overcome obstacles that stand in your way, and make the biggest impact in the world you can make.

STEP 2

DISCOVER YOUR SUPERPOWERS TO OVERCOME CHALLENGES

BEND AND NOT BREAK WITH RESILIENCE

No one escapes pain, fear, and suffering. Yet from pain can come wisdom,
from fear can come courage, from suffering can come strength—
if we have the virtue of resilience.—Eric Greitens

In the summer of 2015, I was diagnosed with bi-lateral breast cancer. This news came out of left field. I couldn't recall a history of breast cancer on either side of my family tree.

Most people I knew who experienced chemo treatments stayed in bed in a dark room for three to four days after their treatment. I couldn't afford to do that. I had a lot of responsibilities going on.

Three years earlier, we opened my husband's new business in San Antonio and Austin. I was busy driving back and forth to our Austin location to supervise our staff, in addition to handling staff development and operations for both locations. My husband handled sales and marketing and he was out of the office most of the time. How was I going to handle chemo treatments and continue to keep up with all my duties?

My oncologist understood my dilemma. She offered some of her patients half-dose chemo treatments over six months, instead of full doses over three months, depending on their extenuating circumstances. I cheerily said, "Sign me up!"

We celebrated my last chemo treatment on December 31, 2015, but shortly after, I started getting out of breath more frequently. When I began my seven weeks of daily radiation, I had to use a walking cane because I would get winded walking from the parking lot to the clinic which was not far. Most of the time I was dropped off at the front entrance but still had difficulty walking and breathing.

My doctor scheduled my double mastectomy three months later. They admitted me into the hospital a few days before my scheduled surgery to eliminate the fluid retained around my heart which caused my breathing problems.

The day before my surgery, my husband entered my hospital room with our son Grigory, who was 19 at the time. My husband wanted me to talk with him about his recent poor behavior because my husband wasn't getting through to him.

Grigory was going through a difficult time and kept to himself. We learned he spent time with unknown people who became a bad influence on him. We suspected he started doing drugs. We were concerned and struggled to get Grigory to open up to us.

The last thing I said to Grigory before he and my husband left my hospital room to return home was "There is nothing you could ever do to make us stop loving you. We don't like this bad behavior. We know you can do the right thing. I love you and I'll talk to you later."

Hours later, my husband returned to my hospital room. When he walked into my room, I saw a couple of nurses waiting outside my door. I noticed his face looked like he had been crying. "Is something wrong?" I asked with a puzzled look on my face.

He looked at me with tears in his eyes and quietly said, "Grigory died by suicide. He's gone."

The next few minutes were a blur. I remember sitting in my hospital bed staring straight ahead. I guess I was in shock because I could not even cry or speak.

One nurse finally asked me if I would like a sedative and I replied quietly "No, thank you." The other nurse asked me if I wanted to reschedule my double mastectomy for another day. I quietly replied "No. Postponing the surgery I already dreaded wouldn't bring Grigory back. Let's get it over with."

Later that day, our Pastor and his wife came to comfort us. They understood what we were going through because they had gone through the same experience years earlier. We talked and cried together.

I knew in my heart that Grigory was in Heaven with my three babies and that I would see them all again. He was at peace. Losing him hurt so much, but I clung to the hope of seeing him again in Heaven, just as God promises.

BITTER OR BETTER

Adversity leaves you bitter or better. It's important to acknowledge your pain so you can process your emotions.

We will all face adversity in our lives. Some people will face it more frequently than others, and some people will have more tragic situations than others.

Regardless of the frequency or degree of hardship, we all have one thing in common: we all get to choose how we respond to it. Will adversity leave you bitter or better? Will you become a victim or a victor?

YOU ALWAYS HAVE CHOICES

As young children, we don't get to make a lot of our own choices because we haven't had enough experiences to learn rewards and consequences. Young children don't know what they don't know. Time and experience teach us that. Life is an adventure and children want to experience it all because it's new and exciting.

As adults, our experiences taught us what's good and what's bad. Some people learn to become overly cautious with life and some learn to keep chasing the next adventure.

One thing remains the same. We still have choices. In a previous chapter, we learned three things we always have in our control: our thoughts, our words, and our actions.

When adversity hits, we can choose to be a victim of our circumstance, or we can choose to be a victor and use our resilience to bend but not break.

WHAT IS RESILIENCE?

Resilience is adapting to new circumstances, making decisions based on facts not emotions, capitalizing on available resources, and believing that you can turn an accident into good fortune. You can adapt and overcome.

Don't worry if you can't do that right now. Resilience is a muscle you must strengthen. "Strengthen?" you ask. Yes, resilience can't be taught; you have to experience it. It is applying theory in real time. "Wait! What?" you gasp. "Are you telling me it's trial by fire?"

Yes, but you've been dealing with obstacles throughout your life and you're still here today. They might not be major life events, but they *were* challenges. When you were a toddler, did you decide one day that you would start walking without falling? Of course not! You practiced standing up by holding on to something and then took a step or two. As your legs became stronger, you could take more steps without falling. Maybe you fell and bumped your head or your knee, but you didn't give up. That's resilience.

As you got older, you experienced more obstacles in life, in school and probably in extra-curricular activities. Maybe you weren't good at one activity, but it led you to try another activity you would have never thought about trying. One activity that you now excel in. That's resilience. You didn't give up. You persevered and looked for new opportunities to succeed.

BE RESILIENT LIKE A PALM TREE

You might be thinking, "A palm tree? Really? Palm trees make me think of tropical drinks and beaches. How are they resilient?"

Palm trees bending during high winds.

Palm trees are the most resilient of trees. They have a genetic make-up that allows them to be very flexible. Even in hurricane winds, palm trees have the capacity to bend almost double without breaking or being uprooted. After the high winds have passed, the palm tree will pop back up into its original position as if nothing happened.

Other trees can snap in two like toothpicks and large oak trees are uprooted easily, but the palm tree stands strong amid the destruction surrounding it. A palm tree's root system is strengthened, not weakened, as a result of severe storms.

EIGHT PRINCIPLES THAT AFFECT YOUR RESILIENCY

Things happen for a reason. No matter how chaotic it may seem, if you persevere, you will find a better opportunity around the corner.

In his book *The Resilience Advantage*, Al Siebert, PhD, shares research that shows how inwardly guided, self-motivated people excel in circumstances of constant change. Attitudes and beliefs play a key role in how resilient they are. Siebert lists eight principles affecting resiliency.

How much do the following statements reflect your beliefs?

1. When hit by life-disrupting change, you will never be the same again. You will emerge either stronger or weaker, either better or bitter. You have within you the ability to determine which way it will be for you.

2. As you struggle with adversity or disruptive change, your mind and your habits will create barriers or bridges to a better future.

3. Blaming others for how bad things are for you keeps you in a non-resilient victim state in which you do not take resilient actions.

4. Life isn't fair, and that can be very good for you. Resiliency comes from feeling personally responsible to find a solution to overcome adversity. Your struggle to bounce back and recover from setbacks can lead to developing strengths and abilities you didn't know you were capable of.

5. Your unique resilient strengths develop from self-motivated, self-managed learning in the school of life.

6. Self-knowledge enhances your resiliency because your way of being resilient must be your own self-created, unique version. Self-knowledge comes from self-observation, experimenting, and being receptive to feedback of all kinds.

7. The observing place within you is where you develop conscious choices about how you will interact with the world you live in. Experiencing choices leads to feelings of freedom, independence, and being in control of your life.

8. As you become more and more resilient, you effectively handle disruptive change, adversities, and major setbacks faster and easier.

CHARACTERISTICS OF RESILIENT PEOPLE

Resilient people are victors and survivors. They faced the odds against them and did it anyway. Resilient people have common characteristics.

Characteristics of a survivor are the ability to dig deep down and find ways to cope during adversity and eventually find the gift that is left behind. Surviving hardship includes a certain mindset, flexibility, and focus on positive goals. A survivor is resilient in distressing circumstances and makes things turn out well.

YOUR ATTITUDE DETERMINES YOUR SURVIVAL

According to Siebert in his book *The Survivor Personality*, "Our attitudes determine our well-being more than our circumstances." Some people thrive in the same adversity that others find overwhelming. You might not have control over your situation, but you have control over your thoughts.

Survivor characteristics develop out of everyday habits that strengthen your coping skills and your chances of survival, should it become necessary. For example, if you must adhere to strict deadlines at work each month, then you know your focus and concentration increases the closer your deadline approaches. You realize you can't let yourself get distracted or you'll miss your deadline. This same focus and concentration come in handy in an unexpected emergency.

SURVIVORS ARE MENTALLY AND EMOTIONALLY FLEXIBLE

According to Siebert, an important trait of survivors is their adaptability or flexibility in any situation. They are not one way or the other. Survivors are both one way *and* the other.

For example, most people are either optimistic or pessimistic, Type A or Type B personality, and extroverted or introverted. However, survivors can be both. Having *biphasic personality traits* increases the ability to survive in any situation or fall somewhere in between the two extremes. The longer the list of opposing traits, the more complex you are. The more complex, the more adaptable to deal successfully with whatever situation develops.

Adaptation is the key to survival. People who can't handle life well usually have one way of acting in all situations. The survivor, instead, thinks that their personality traits are a function of how they choose to interact with the situation they are in. Survivors adapt and overcome their circumstances.

SURVIVORS ARE GOOD TROUBLESHOOTERS

Survivors are good troubleshooters because they are handy and creative, and they develop easy solutions to difficult problems. They want and need things to work smoothly and easily. Fortunately, they possess the common sense to make that happen.

Synergy is their primary motivation in life. Survivors are not prone to complaining. If something isn't working well, they feel the urge to make improvements. Their goal is a win/win situation.

According to Siebert, the following is a list of ways you can become more synergistic:

- In difficult situations, ask yourself "How can I interact with this situation, so things work out for everyone involved?"
- Look for creative ways for things to work out well by asking those involved for their input to a positive solution.
- Search for ways to convert obstacles into opportunities to make things work better.
- Develop a personal code of moral principles and ethical practices.

One way to recognize you are developing a synergistic nature is that you accomplish more with less effort.

SURVIVORS HAVE A TALENT FOR SERENDIPITY

Survivors can turn obstacles into opportunities. Adversity can take your life in a different and better direction than you could have imagined. Serendipity is not good luck or a lucky accident, it's transforming hardship into growth.

- Highly resilient people can turn a life-disruptive event into a gift through creativity. Your ability to turn hardship into growth allows you to discover strengths you didn't know you had.
- When looking for the gift from adversity, hunt for the good stuff. Ask yourself "What good can come out of this?" Look at the situation from all angles.

- Change is hard, but it can lead to new opportunities you would not have pursued if things remained the same.

SURVIVORS ADAPT TO NEW REALITIES QUICKLY

Survivors adapt to new realities by being aware of their surroundings. They notice clues that something or someone is out of place. The quick scan of a critical situation includes a fast read of what people are doing and then act or react immediately. The more quickly a person assesses the complete picture of what is happening, the better their chance of survival.

When faced with a crisis, survivors can regulate their emotions and not panic. Panic is just an emotional response that interferes with logical thought processes and lessens your chance of survival. Survivors set their emotions aside and can quickly evaluate the facts.

10 TIPS TO DEVELOP A SURVIVOR PERSONALITY

1. **Ask questions.** Developing your curiosity for new situations increases your ability to understand the big picture of what is happening.
2. **Increase your emotional and mental flexibility**. Tap into your biphasic personality traits in different situations. Survivors are flexible and adapt to their circumstances.
3. **Accept that change with uncertainty is a way of life.** Change is going to happen. Commit to hunting the good in every situation. If you look for opportunities in hardship, you will find them.
4. **Learn from all experiences.** Failures differ from mistakes. Failure is when you stop trying. Mistakes are lessons learned from how not to do something.
5. **Develop empathy.** Put yourself in someone else's shoes. Look at the situation from their eyes and understand what they see and feel about how they want the issue to be resolved. Look for the win/win solution so things work out for everyone involved.

6. **Avoid labeling people.** Labels reinforce the perception of someone's behavior and restricts you to see their ability to change. Instead of saying someone is a jerk, say someone is acting like a jerk. Address their behavior, not their character.

7. **Make time to observe and reflect.** Take time to scan your surroundings and observe what is happening around you. Set your emotions aside and reflect on the facts. Do you see red flags or warning clues?

8. **Find ways to be useful in situations.** Survivors like synergy. What can you do so things work out well for all involved? Your ability to be useful in a situation makes you valuable and valued.

9. **Appreciate yourself.** Your self-esteem determines how much you learn in difficult situations. The stronger your self-esteem, the more you learn.

10. **Follow the survive and thrive sequence.** Balance your emotions, adapt and cope in your immediate situation, thrive by learning and improving the situation for those involved, and then find the gift in your hardship.

THE REST OF MY STORY

After I went through the grieving process, I chose to focus on Grigory's achievements and the happy memories we shared over the past ten years together. He did enjoy a happy childhood with us. I believed God's promises were true. I would see Grigory again in Heaven, which gave me joy and hope.

Shortly after Grigory's death, one of his former Boy Scout Leaders, also his *second mom*, contacted me to pass on a story about Grigory helping a younger Boy Scout in our troop.

Over the years, Justin and Grigory, both Eagle Scouts, were very active in their troop. Justin, the extrovert, served in leadership roles while Grigory, the introvert, preferred smaller roles in helping the new, younger Scouts work on their merit badges.

One of the new boys mentioned to Grigory that he really wanted to become an Eagle Scout but probably wouldn't achieve it. Grigory told him if he participated in the weekly meetings, weekend campouts, and worked on his merit badges, then he could achieve the rank of Eagle Scout. Every week, the boy would show up to the meetings ready to work on his merit badges with Grigory.

The same boy recounted this story at his Eagle Scout Ceremony shortly after Grigory's death. He said if it wasn't for Grigory's encouragement, he wouldn't be receiving his Eagle Scout rank. You never know what impact you can have on someone when you show them a little kindness.

Another impact Grigory's death had in our community was as an organ donor. Someone received the gift of sight when they received Grigory's corneas. The local Eye Bank sent us a beautiful memorial coin that we cherish and keep with his mementos.

Because of our adoption experience, and to honor Grigory's memory, I became a mentor with a local non-profit organization that bridges the gap between foster care and adulthood for youth who age out of the foster care system.

You *can* transform pain into growth and become a survivor. With each adversity, your toolbox of resilience skills grows, and you become mentally and emotionally stronger. A difficulty that initially almost broke your spirit can become one of the best things that ever happened to you.

* * *

In the next chapter, you will discover your superpowers and how to leverage them to strengthen resilience and overcome any challenge.

EXERCISE: PUT IT IN ACTION

1. As you read over the Eight Principles That Affect Your Resiliency, did you reflect on how relevant they are to you? How much or how little do you believe they are true?
2. From the 10 Tips to Develop a Survivor Personality, pick five or more tips and list specific actions you can take to build your resilience.

DISCOVER YOUR SUPERPOWERS

*A hero is an ordinary individual who finds the strength to persevere
and endure in spite of overwhelming obstacles.*
—Christopher Reeve

Two years into my husband's new business, we had staff turnover, which was bittersweet. We realized our employees needed certain characteristics, specifically dependable, reliable, and being proactive instead of reactive. Our reputation for excellent customer service was important to us.

My husband was familiar with the ins-and-outs of this business industry, but I was not. I learned from the ground up through hours of research and questioning our vendors about their processes so that I could train our staff properly.

My past work experience included accounting and business operations. I wore many hats in the beginning of our business: office manager, accounting manager, staff trainer, customer service manager, and human resource manager. This allowed my husband to focus on sales and marketing for the growth of our business.

We started with two staff members at each of our San Antonio and Austin locations but was down to one staff member at each location. They required a lot of supervision—more than I could handle by myself.

At the time, my husband served in the Army National Guard and received orders for a three-week deployment with his unit to Africa. We decided when he returned, we would replace our two remaining employees.

Since I had to learn my husband's business from the ground up, I knew I could train anyone to do the job, if they were motivated to learn. Our current employees had lost their desire, and our clients were noticing.

During the first week of my husband's deployment, my twin sister, who was living with us, had major surgery, and was recovering at a skilled nursing facility next to the hospital by our home. I would visit her daily on my way home to see if she needed anything.

At the end of the first week, on Sunday night, my employee in Austin texted me stating he quit. No explanation and no response to my reply, "Why?" After looking around the office Monday morning, I concluded that he hadn't followed customer protocol the previous Friday and didn't want to be held accountable for his error.

A week later, my remaining employee in San Antonio quit after I discovered he reloaded his personal video game, after I deleted it the first time, on our office computer. Evidently, he found the stern note I left him the night before stating that playing his personal video game on our office computer was not acceptable when there was a stack of paperwork that needed to be entered. After he quit, I spent over 20 hours putting two weeks' worth of paperwork into the computer.

So, during the third and final week of my husband's deployment to Africa, I was our only "employee" working at both locations, 65 miles apart.

I worked the mornings in San Antonio, closed the office at lunch, and quickly drove the hour and a half trip to work in our Austin location in the afternoon. After closing, I caught up on that day's paperwork for both locations, then drove the hour and a half trip back to San Antonio.

On my way home, usually around 10 p.m., I'd stop by the skilled nursing facility to visit my sister and see how she was doing before I went home. I crawled into bed around midnight and repeated this schedule for the rest of the week. I was so happy that our offices were closed on the weekends so I could catch up on the rest of the week's paperwork and my sleep!

I truly felt like Wonder Woman during those three weeks. I never knew what I was capable of doing until I was faced with so many challenges in such a short time. I had to push onward for our customers, our business, and most importantly, for my family.

Giving up was never an option.

SUPERPOWERS

A superpower gives you confidence to push aside fear and tackle the challenges in front of you.

What is your superpower? Mine is resilience! I'm able to overcome adversity in a single bound!

Okay, not exactly in a single bound. But over the past 30 years, I've learned that I can bend and not break. I never knew how flexible I could be until I was put to the test.

If you told me I would get through that three-week experience, I'd laugh and tell you no way. I'm not that tough. But I did get through many difficult experiences, and I became stronger from it.

It's not about what I've done, but what God has done through me. I wouldn't have overcome so many challenges in my life if not for the power of the Holy Spirit. I'm just an ordinary person doing extraordinary things through Him who gives me strength.

One thing I can say about my adversities is that I am a better person because of what I've been through. I know what my strengths are and when I need to turn to resources or ask for help. I have more purpose and meaning in my life because of growth and gratitude. My situations were difficult, but I knew they could have been much worse. Fortunately, they weren't.

I've learned to persevere over long periods of time and not give up. It wasn't easy because sometimes I had few options in my control. These hardships helped me trust in my Lord and Savior to carry me through the most difficult time. I don't want any regrets or wonder *"Should I have done this..."* or *"If only I had done that..."* Solving problems became easier when I discovered how to think creatively. I'll go into more detail on these topics later in the book.

Everything I'm teaching you is what I've put into practice, through trial and error, over the past 30 years. Fortunately, you don't have to figure it out on your own or wait years to learn it. You can implement the concepts in this book right now and begin to change your situation for the better.

WHAT ARE SUPERPOWERS?

Superpowers are made up of your skills, talents, passions, and character strengths. In other words, your personal assets.

When was the last time you took an assessment of what makes you *you*? What are your accomplishments from birth to now? What difficulties have you overcome in the past? What topics or reasons do people come to you for advice?

To discover your superpowers, let's take an inventory of your personal assets.

SKILLS

A skill is an ability to perform an activity in a competent manner. Skills can include soft/hard skills, transferable/functional skills, interpersonal skills, professional and personal skills, and many others. Some examples include:

- *Communication:* an active listener, good verbal and written skills
- *Time Management:* effectively manages one's time, organized, meets deadlines
- *Teamwork:* recognizes strengths and weaknesses of team members, puts project's success ahead of personal gain
- *Organization:* organizes time, tasks, and a schedule so things get done in the right order and efficiently
- *Interpersonal:* comfortable and compatible with all sorts of people, adjusts communication style as needed
- *Critical Thinking:* takes an analytical approach to problems, streamlines processes for efficiency
- *Dependable:* someone whom people can turn to for help in any type of situation
- *Self-motivated:* takes initiative to succeed in tasks or goals
- and many more…

TALENTS

Talents come naturally to an individual and are abilities that result from learning, development, and disciplined practice. It's an activity that you excel in. A few examples are:

- Playing a musical instrument
- Excelling in a sport
- Writing
- Teaching
- Painting
- Problem-Solving
- Storytelling
- and many more...

PASSIONS

A passion is something that holds significant meaning to you or an activity that you enjoy doing. When you practice your passions, you bring greater fulfillment to your life.

You can go after your passions now and not wait until you reach retirement age. Volunteering is a great way to find like-minded people who share your passions.

If time and money were no object, what would you love to do that you're passionate about? Open a café or an art studio? Teach children to play chess or teach a theater class? Write fiction books or a screenplay? Paint landscapes or design landscapes?

CHARACTER STRENGTHS

In their book *The Power of Character Strength*, Ryan M. Niemiec, PsyD, and Robert E. McGrath, PhD, explain that character is the part of your personality that other people tend to admire, respect, and cherish.

Their research, sponsored by the VIA Institute on Character, discovered there are 24 central character strengths in human beings, each falling under larger categories called virtues. Niemiec and McGrath named this the VIA Classification of Character Strengths and Virtues.

When the VIA Classification was developed, the connections between strengths and virtues weren't perfect since a strength can reflect more than one virtue and some strengths are more connected to one specific virtue than another.

Unlike skills and talents, character strengths cut straight to the core of who you are. When things are going well, you can use character strengths to help see what is best in yourself and others. When things are going poorly, you can use your character strengths to give balance to the challenges you face to avoid becoming too self-critical.

Reflecting on your strengths can help offset negative experiences and remind you that you have unique resources available. Studies show that when you make the most of your character strengths, you become happier, more productive, and more engaged in what you're doing.

Virtue of Wisdom - Strengths that help you gather and use knowledge

- *Creativity:* flexible, resourceful, finds different ways of doing things
- *Curiosity*: attentive, examines, seeks innovation
- *Judgment/Critical Thinking:* logical, factual, analytical
- *Love of Learning:* masters new skills, adds to knowledge
- *Perspective:* knowledgeable, gives wise advice, sees big picture

Virtue of Courage - Strengths that help you exercise your will and face adversity

- *Bravery:* courageous, faces fears, heroic
- *Perseverance:* resilient, completes what is started, diligent
- *Honesty:* trustworthy, credible, honorable
- *Zest:* loves life, energetic, intentional

Virtue of Humanity - Strengths that help you in one-on-one relationships

- *Love:* able to love and be loved, adoration, cherishes

- *Kindness:* compassionate, generous, nurturing
- *Social Intelligence:* emotionally intelligent, reads people well, understands social cues

Virtue of Justice - Strengths that help you in community or group-based situations

- *Teamwork*: commits to group efforts, loyal, collaborates
- *Fairness:* adheres to justice, equity, non-bias
- *Leadership:* leads to get things done, guides positively, resourceful

Virtue of Temperance - Strengths that help you manage habits and protect against excess

- *Forgiveness*: shows mercy, compassion, offers second chances
- *Humility:* humble, modest, lets actions speak for themselves
- *Prudence:* cautious, careful, avoids risks
- *Self-Regulation:* disciplined, manages emotions and impulses

Virtue of Transcendence - Strengths that help you connect to the larger universe and provide meaning

- *Appreciation of Beauty and Excellence*: awe and wonder for beauty, admires skills and excellence in others
- *Gratitude:* appreciative, thankful, feels blessed
- *Hope*: optimistic, expects best and works to achieve it
- *Humor:* playful, brings smiles to others, sees the lighter side
- *Spirituality:* beliefs about the meaning of life that shape conduct and provide comfort

PUTTING IT ALL TOGETHER

In the previous chapter, we talked about strengthening your resilience so you can bend and not break when you experience adversity. Another way to strengthen your resilience is taking an inventory of your personal assets: skills, talents, passions, and character strengths. These are some of your resources to call on and use creatively when obstacles arise.

Think back over your life and make a list of challenges you've overcome. They can be related to school, employment, health, finances, community activities, or whatever. Accomplishments can be small, average, or huge.

What skills, talents, passions, and character strengths helped you overcome those challenges? Be specific. Do you see any patterns that stand out?

Keep this list handy to refer to while you read the rest of this book, and especially when you are having a rough day or week. You have what it takes to overcome obstacles because you can call on your superpowers.

CREATE YOUR MANTRA FOR RESILIENCE

A mantra is a short, key phrase that can be memorized and repeated for positivity and motivation. Mantras can give you courage to break through limiting beliefs and achieve your true potential. Below are a few examples.

- Good things come to those who wait.
- Stop and smell the roses.
- There's no time like the present.
- Forget the mistake, remember the lesson.
- I will figure it out.
- If you want something different, do something different.
- Keep it simple.

One way to practice your resilience skills is to create mantras.

Let's go back to the previous chapters in which we talked about characteristics of resilient people. What characteristics, skills, or principles of resiliency do you need to implement in your life?

When I was recovering from heart transplant surgery while going through my divorce, I came up with several mantras that I would say to myself whenever I felt things weren't going well or felt my life was spinning out of control.

- **Daily Mantra:** Hunt the good stuff, find the humor, stay positive, and focus on my blessings.
- **Emergency Mantra:** I can't do that, but I can do this, and I will do it now.
- **Reality Mantra:** I am grateful that it's not worse because I could be experiencing _____.
- **Perseverance Mantra:** I will persevere and get through this by focusing on what's in my control to change, which is _____.

The purpose of creating these mantras is to remind yourself that you can find a way to get through any difficult situation because you have choices. Each time you say a mantra out loud or to yourself, you are strengthening your resilience. Just like the palm tree bending in high winds, you will bend and not break because you are resilient.

Remember, you are in control of your thoughts, your words, and your actions.

THE REST OF MY STORY

During my challenging week of being our only employee, my teenage sons stepped up and helped me by taking care of themselves. Thank goodness my boys were old enough to drive and get to their part-time job where they both worked. Depending on their schedules, one would drop the other off at their sport practice and get to their practice just in time.

Those three weeks that my husband was out of the country were some of the toughest times of my life. I persevered and held onto hope. God gave me the strength I needed to make it through each day. How true is the scripture verse Philippians 4:13 (ESV): "I can do all things through Him who strengthens me."

I learned a lot about my resilience and watched my creative problem-solving skills improve. These skills would help me overcome future challenges in my life.

EXERCISE: PUT IT IN ACTION

1. Make a list of your assets or superpowers: skills, talents, passions, and character strengths.
2. How did your superpowers help you overcome obstacles in your past? Did that give you more confidence?
3. If you are currently going through difficulties, how can you use your superpowers in new ways to help you move forward?

THE iCOPE PROBLEM SOLVING METHOD

There are no big problems, there are just a lot of little problems.
—Henry Ford

The year 2020 was the best year of my life and the worst year of my life.

In January, my heart doctors diagnosed me with genetic Congestive Heart Failure (CHF). Because of my heart's deterioration, they informed me I would need a heart transplant very soon. The CHF was triggered by my chemo treatments five years prior.

The heart transplant was bittersweet news to me. On one hand, I was so tired of struggling to breathe that I welcomed it, and on the other hand, a heart transplant terrified me. I didn't know anyone who experienced a heart transplant.

It had become so hard to breathe. Sometimes at night, I tried to sleep slumped over a big pillow in my rocking chair in the living room. It was hard to breathe when lying down in my bed or on the couch.

Since I could only take shallow breaths, I had to close my eyes and completely relax my body so I could take one deep breath. If I couldn't get that deep breath on the first try, I tried not to panic trying to get it on the second or third try. I realized having a heart transplant was less scary than the fear of not being able to breathe. I was ready to start the process of getting on that heart transplant list.

As I went through a plethora of tests to qualify for the heart transplant list, my husband and I attended several educational sessions at the heart clinic to understand the risks involved with the surgery.

In my mind, there were only two options: 1) my heart transplant would be a success so my quality of life would greatly improve, or 2) I wouldn't make it through the surgery, and I would live pain free in Heaven. It never occurred to me that there was a third possibility: I survive the surgery, but with complications.

The palliative nurse's presentation opened my eyes to a lot of "What if...?" scenarios that I'd never considered. Palliative care is treatment of the discomfort, symptoms, and stress of a serious illness. This type of treatment can help improve the patient's quality of life and help caregivers and family as well.

My husband and I had to consider and discuss worse case scenarios if complications arose. I had to identify what the deal breaker would be for my quality of life. Those were very difficult conversations to have. I prayed many prayers that God would just give me options one or two during my surgery.

* * *

One month after learning I needed a heart transplant, our 83-year-old father passed away, and we had his memorial service in March, a week before COVID shut down everything. Family and friends recommended I not attend his memorial service because of my high risk of infection, but I needed to be there. My father was such a loving, caring, and humble man. It brought me such joy to listen to the wonderful memories and stories from his dear friends.

* * *

On April 20, 2020, I entered the hospital to await my new heart. Because of COVID, new protocols were in place, which meant no visitors were allowed.

I was told that it might take a while to find the right tissue match, especially during the pandemic, so I came prepared with my laptop and continued to work from my hospital bed.

I expected to wait four to six weeks to find a good match. At least I could video chat with our work staff, family, and friends. Under these dire circumstances, I would be okay. The hospital staff took such good care of me that I felt like royalty.

Six days later, my doctor rushed into my hospital room to tell me he was on his way to the airport to look at a new heart that came in and verify it was a good match for me. It was a good match, and I received my new heart a few hours later!

It was a miracle. My blood type was O positive, which is very common on the transplant lists. It's good to have O positive when donating blood, but for transplant *recipients*, it's better to have an uncommon blood type like AB negative to limit the competition for the same organ. However, God was looking after me once again because my doctors were amazed the heart was a perfect match for me!

The first week after my surgery, I looked like a sci-fi experiment with many tubes pushing fluids into my body and pulling other fluids out of my body. As soon as I came out of the anesthesia, they had me sitting in a chair as much as I could.

At first, I had to have two nurses help me stand up because my legs had no strength. They forbid me to use my arms because of my chest incision. I was given a big, beautiful, heart-shaped pillow to hug while the nurses helped me stand up and sit down. A group of special volunteers handmade these heart pillows for the cardiac patients. A week later, I only needed one nurse's help, and a few days later I could rock back and forth in the chair and stand up on my own while hugging my precious heart pillow.

My recovery exceeded everyone's expectations. The biggest miracle was that I experienced absolutely no pain after the surgery. My medical team was surprised that I didn't need any pain medication.

Two weeks after my surgery, they discharged me in time for Mother's Day weekend. What a joyful time to celebrate with my family! As my nurse wheeled me down to the front entrance of the hospital where my husband was waiting with the car, I chuckled and said to her, "I can't imagine going through anything more challenging than a heart transplant."

* * *

Looking back, I see why God took such good care of me during my heart transplant surgery. He gave me a phenomenal heart transplant team. God knew I would need to be reminded again that He can get me through any challenge, no matter how difficult it is.

After the first month of recovering at home, I indeed faced a bigger challenge. I discovered my husband was having an affair with a woman he'd hired the previous year to help him with his second business. In fact, he talked me into hiring her to help him with our business. I felt devastated, confused, angry, hurt, and betrayed. I was on an emotional rollercoaster, and I couldn't get off. *How could my husband choose this other relationship over our marriage of 27 years?*

I moved in with my twin sister and continued my heart transplant recovery at her place since she was working from home during COVID. I contacted our former marriage counselor for individual counseling because she knew our marriage history.

During the divorce process, I learned that my husband's affair had begun earlier than I thought. I realized why he had moved on from our marriage so quickly; the affair started almost two years prior. Reconciliation was not an option. I had to radically accept the end of my marriage and build a new life for myself at age 58.

Our divorce became final five months later. Just like that, twenty-eight years together ended. I felt like a failure. I felt humiliated. I didn't want to be another divorce statistic. I certainly didn't want to be labeled a middle-aged divorcee whose husband left her for another woman. I felt tossed aside like an old rag doll.

I went through the grief stages. When I experienced the anger stage, I was ready to accept my divorce and move on with my new life. I had a new heart and a second chance at life. I was excited to start living my new life!

* * *

I had a wonderful Christian counselor to help me process my wide range of emotions during the divorce and focus on my heart transplant recovery. She reminded me the Bible says I'm fearfully and wonderfully made. I am chosen. I am a child of God. In other words, "God don't make no junk!" (Ignore the double negative.) I am worthy. God is with me, just like he was through my successful heart transplant. He knew this was coming and that I needed to trust him again. He had plans for me. I had hope that I would persevere and overcome this very difficult situation.

I focused on what was in my control to change. What was out of my control would get turned over to my all-powerful and all-knowing God. I wondered where the Holy Spirit would lead me. I knew it had to be good because God promises to bring good out of every situation.

Regardless of the COVID restrictions, my heart doctors told me I must quarantine for a year at home to ensure no infections or rejection of my new heart. This quarantine left me very little options for finding a job. I would have to be creative to solve this problem.

TOO MANY PROBLEMS

Problems can range from small, such as what to cook for dinner, to large, like losing a loved one unexpectedly.

Problem solving refers to the mental process you go through to discover, analyze, and solve problems. Before problem solving can happen, it is imperative to first understand the exact nature of the situation. If you're unclear about the problem, your attempts to resolve it will be incorrect or flawed.

Studies show that individuals who become extremely emotional in the middle of adversity do not cope well with handling difficult situations. Not that reacting emotionally is wrong; it is just that this type of person responds emotionally at the worst possible time and place. Negative emotions decrease resiliency. This person might simply wait for a problem to go away on its own, only prolonging the difficult circumstance.

Understanding why the problem happened reveals two courses of action: 1) you radically accept the situation and move on with your life; or 2) you identify and resolve the root cause of the problem. Both courses of action involve changing what's in your control.

It's important to realize that *not* making a decision is still a decision. The problem will hang around and continue to cause you stress and anxiety. Trust me, you don't want that because you will catastrophize into the pit of despair. This will only bring on more feelings of helplessness and hopelessness.

Instead, start working toward solving your problems. While there may not be any fast or simple solution, you can take baby steps toward improving your situation and decreasing your stress.

THREE TYPES OF INTELLIGENCE USED TO SOLVE PROBLEMS

In *The Resiliency Advantage*, Siebert discusses three kinds of intelligence used by people in almost every culture.

1. **Analytical:** Rational, problem-solving skills involve analysis, logic, and reasoning to solve familiar problems. Identify the problem, state the desired goal, collect information, consider several solutions, take action, and evaluate the results. Develop this type of problem solving by applying these skills to daily challenges.

2. **Creative:** This kind of intelligence is used to create unusual solutions in new and unfamiliar circumstances. Your conscious mind is like the tip of an iceberg protruding out of a vast ocean rich with a lifetime of cumulative information. Creative problem solving begins with the feeling that a new, unconventional solution is possible.

3. **Practical:** This type of problem solving applies to situational, real-life problems. It can be a hybrid of analytical and creative problem solving used by people who also call it "street smarts". Many people without higher education are successful in life because they are very practical in how they handle the world they live in.

The ingenuity to discover a clever solution to a problem comes from thinking outside of the box of old perceptions, assumptions, and traditional ways of thinking. It may also result from having emotional independence drawn from a group of people all experiencing similar difficulties.

The important prerequisite for problem solving real-life challenges is the ability to accept the reality of what is happening and do so without the emotions of feeling distraught or furious about what people have done to disrupt your life. (Review Radical Acceptance in Chapter 1.)

Resilience studies show that individuals who survive extreme difficulties fully embrace what is happening. You may not like it, but you accept those circumstances, rather than erupting with anger or finding blame for what has happened. The more you fight against it and argue with the new reality, the more trapped you will become with feelings of helplessness and energy-wasting activities.

BENEFITS OF GOOD PROBLEM-SOLVING SKILLS

When you are skilled at problem solving, it can prepare you with solutions for problems that might occur down the road. Effective problem solving develops self-confidence and strengthens resiliency, which also leads to better health. This two-way connection empowers you to live your life in a manner that allows you to enjoy many pleasurable moments, which in turn increases your problem-solving skills.

FOCUS ON FACTS INSTEAD OF EMOTIONS

Critical thinking is logical reasoning. It takes emotion out of a situation and analyzes and evaluates known facts. In problem solving, this is a vital skill used to make informed decisions instead of having impulsive reactions. Developing this reasoning skill is easy; you do it daily without realizing it.

When problems arise, it's easy to jump to conclusions like the fictional character Chicken Little who yelled, "The sky is falling! The sky is falling!" when a bird flying overhead dropped an acorn on his head.

Instead of jumping to conclusions based on your emotions, ask yourself, *"What are the facts in this situation?"* Do you know enough facts to make an informed decision, or do you have time to collect more information?

Critical thinking explores different perspectives of the same problem. Be open-minded and look at the situation from all angles. Additional perspectives could uncover pertinent facts that might not be seen from a single point of view. A good example is looking at eyewitness statements from the same car accident. The witnesses' accounts will be a little different based on where they were standing when they saw the accident happen.

Critical thinking pursues the different resources available to you. Think outside of the box to identify the people, information, products, and services needed to make an educated decision. You don't have to know all the information to make a decision, but it certainly helps if you know how to access resources when a timely decision is needed.

Like a good detective, exercise critical thinking by asking questions to understand. For example, I'm a "why" person and I like to ask questions out of curiosity to understand a situation. If I don't feel comfortable asking someone my question, then I may do my own research to see if the problem has a solution.

The more you engage your critical thinking skills to make informed decisions, the more confidence you have to resolve the problem. If you made it through one hardship, then you can get through another. Having hope is action-oriented and enables you to keep pushing forward.

5 STEPS TO SUCCESSFUL PROBLEM SOLVING

The iCOPE 5-Step Problem Solving Method walks you through the decision-making process by using the acronym **iCOPE**. I'll give you the overview, and then we'll dive deeper into the details.

1. **IDENTIFY** the problem to solve that will have the greatest impact to move you forward toward your goal.
2. Make a list of what's in your **CONTROL** to **CHANGE**.
3. Determine the Best and Worst **OUTCOMES** to get to the Most-Likely **OUTCOME**.

4. Decide on a **PLAN** of action to implement the Most-Likely Outcome.

5. **EVALUATE** throughout the process and adjust as necessary.

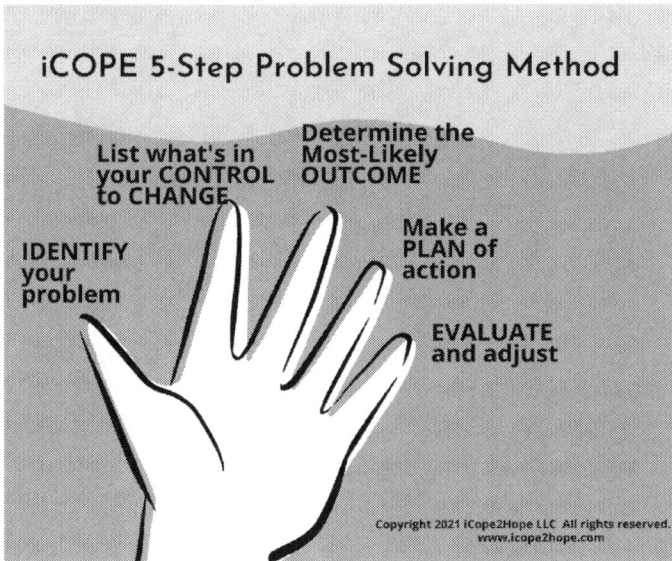

iCOPE 5-Step Problem Solving Method

List what's in your CONTROL to CHANGE

Determine the Most-Likely OUTCOME

IDENTIFY your problem

Make a PLAN of action

EVALUATE and adjust

IDENTIFY

I recommend making a list of one to three small and specific problems that you can resolve in a reasonable time frame, so you gain confidence from seeing progress. When adversity hits, it might be obvious what your top three problems are. If not, start with the main problem and break it down into smaller problems that can be easier to solve. Make sure you have control over the problems you identified.

One way to do this is to get to the root of the problem. You can't solve a problem without uncovering its cause. The faster you identify the true cause, the faster you generate the solution. Why did it happen? Don't play the blame game with excuses. Look at the facts of the situation. Don't go by your emotions.

Pick your first smaller problem to resolve that has the greatest impact on your situation.

In my story above, I identified two problems to solve: 1) reduce the stress from my divorce while recovering from my heart transplant; and 2) find a way to earn revenue from home during my heart transplant quarantine.

CONTROL

Once you have identified the problem with the greatest impact, it's time to determine what is in your control to change.

First, make a list of what's *not* in your control to change. Be specific. Example: You don't have control over what people think or do. Write it down on a piece of paper or even a whiteboard. This will be the only time you think about this because you can't change the unchangeable. This exercise is only used to help you identify where you will not be wasting your time and energy.

Remember, radical acceptance is when you choose to accept what is out of your control. You don't have to approve of it or like it, but you must acknowledge it. You can't change the unchangeable so learn to say, "It is what it is."

Next, make a list of what is in your control to change. This is what you will focus on going forward. Prioritize what you can change by the biggest impact it will have on your situation. Then list the resources available to you, such as people, internet research (websites, articles, videos, etc), community information, etc.

To reduce stress during my heart transplant recovery, I had several things in my control: 1) I could journal my feelings; 2) I could make a list of healthy snacks to prevent stress eating; 3) I could return to daily Bible reading to remind me of God's promise that He's with me always; and 4) I could make a weekly schedule of productive tasks to keep me from ruminating about my divorce. I came up with more, but these had the biggest impact to move forward with my new life.

I had an idea on how to solve my problem of working from home. I wanted to help others struggling to move beyond adversity. I had a lot of experience finding the good in bad situations. I wanted to share my knowledge, resources, and coping skills to help others overcome and flourish after adversity.

OUTCOME

Keep the end in mind. Determine the Best and Worst Outcomes in order to identify the Most-Likely Outcome to resolve your problem.

1. **Best Outcome:** What is your ideal outcome if money and resources were unlimited? There are no obstacles to stand in your way, so brainstorm unlimited possibilities.
2. **Worst Outcome:** What are the worst things that could happen to you if you had no money or resources available? How bad would your situation truly get? Where is your rock bottom?
3. **Most-Likely Outcome:** You're looking at a more realistic outcome somewhere between your best and worst outcomes, which are now your guardrails. What will most likely happen in your life as you resolve your problem?

In my situation above, the most-likely outcome for reducing stress during my heart transplant recovery and divorce proceedings was to walk with my sister in our neighborhood to clear my head and to stick to my whole food, plant-based eating plan to keep my new heart strong and healthy.

PLAN

Now that you have identified your problem, made a list of what's in your control to change, and what you expect the most-likely outcome to be, it's time to map out your plan of action and implement it.

State the problem you have chosen to solve and why it has the most impact in moving you closer to your goal. Write it on paper and tape it to your bathroom mirror, refrigerator, or computer monitor, or put it in your notes app on your phone. Better yet, record a pep talk video you can listen to. This will remind you why you're doing what you're doing, so you don't quit when obstacles arise. Obstacles will arise, but that's when you use your superpowers to overcome them.

List what is in your control to change your situation and the action steps to take. Break it down into smaller tasks with deadlines. Keep it realistic. Baby steps ensure consistency, and achieving your goals increases your confidence. Focus on your accomplishments along the way instead of all the tasks you still need to complete. How do you eat an elephant? One bite at a time.

Be flexible when going after your most-likely outcome; it's not written in stone. The road to success might get bumpy, so keep your eyes on your goal. Reassess what resources you have available to reach your goal. Remind yourself that it could be worse and go over your worst outcome to ensure it's not that bad. Be grateful for each step along the way that gets you closer to your goal.

EVALUATE

Evaluate along the way. You are flexible. You can adapt and overcome obstacles in your path.

Are you making decisions that move you closer to resolving your problem? If not, is your problem too big? Are too many variables out of your control? Are the resources you counted on not available anymore? If any of these statements are true, then go back and identify your problem again. This problem may have to move to your out-of-your-control list.

Are you changing the things in your control by your deadlines? If not, why? Is it fear? What would happen if you changed nothing at all? Do you need to review how to avoid your thinking traps?

Remind yourself WHY you're doing this.

THE REST OF MY STORY

During my divorce, I met the military's requirements for being a 20/20/20 unremarried former spouse. This meant I was eligible for medical benefits under my social security number as well as a small percentage of my ex-husband's Army National Guard retirement pay. It was just enough to cover my half of the living expenses with my sister, There wasn't a problem meeting the requirements, but it was extremely frustrating to get my benefits activated.

After thirteen months of getting the runaround with Army Human Resources Command Headquarters and their local offices in San Antonio, I finally enrolled in my health insurance. No one wanted to tell me what the exact problem was that prevented me from enrolling. I was only told to call one of three departments, who told me to call the other department, who told me to call the other department. I was caught in an endless loop.

I decided to do my own research with U.S. Code Title 10 to show the military I was not giving up on my approved former military spouse benefits. I took copious notes of what each department told me on the phone, I kept all my emails, and documented all my research.

During this thirteen-month process, I paid out-of-pocket for my expensive, monthly prescription drugs that prevented the risk of infection or rejection of my new heart. I couldn't afford to pay out-of-pocket for my remaining four months of lab work, follow-up appointments, or heart biopsies which upset me and my heart doctors immensely.

I was also frustrated when I had to stop my counseling sessions during my divorce which was paid for through my insurance. I tried to focus on the positive things in my life that I could do. I started with practicing gratitude. It was difficult in the beginning but became easier with daily practice.

I believe God's grace and mercy, staying home to quarantine, and eating whole food, plant-based meals, helped me stay healthy and COVID-free during those thirteen months without insurance.

I kept myself busy by journaling daily, reading my Bible, working on my online resilience business, playing the piano again, and crocheting baby blankets for local charities. Despite the frustration with my military benefits, I rediscovered joy and it became a game-changer.

Exercise: Put It in Action

1. Which type of problem solver are you? Analytical, Creative, or Practical? Or a combination? Why?

2. What level are your critical thinking skills? Beginner, Intermediate, or Advanced? Why? What can you do to improve your skills to the next level?

3. Choose a small problem to apply the iCOPE Problem Solving Method.

- **IDENTIFY** your problem and the root cause.
- List what's in your **CONTROL** to **CHANGE** and what's not in your control to change.
- Determine your Best, Worst, and Most-Likely **OUTCOMES**.
- Make a **PLAN** of action that results in the Most-Likely Outcome.
- **EVALUATE** the process and adjust your action plan as needed.

CASE STUDY: LOUIS ZAMPERINI

To persevere, I think, is important for everybody.
Don't give up, don't give in. There's always an answer to everything.
—Louis Zamperini

Louis Zamperini (1917- 2014) was an Olympic athlete and a World War II prisoner of war who later became an inspirational speaker.

Louis Zamperini was always phenomenal. After getting into trouble in his younger years and successfully outrunning the local police, Louis found an outlet in track and field. In a time when the four-minute mile was one of the most sought-after ambitions in sports, Louis pushed the limits. In 1934, at 17, he set the national high school record for the mile with a time of 4:21.3 and held that record for an incredible 20 years.

He attended the University of Southern California on a scholarship and began training for the 1936 Olympics. At the Berlin Olympics, Louis, age 19, finished eighth in the 5000-meter race, but completed the quickest final lap of all the competitors in an unprecedented 56 seconds. His final effort even grabbed the attention of Adolf Hitler, who, after the race, personally congratulated him. Looking back, Louis said he did not know what was coming and regretted meeting the German dictator.

In 1940, Louis graduated from USC and had his sights on winning a gold medal at the 1940 Olympics, but the outbreak of World War II canceled his plans.

Louis enlisted in the Army Air Corps. In 1943, Louis and a crew went out on a flight mission to search for a pilot whose plane had gone down. Their B-24 Liberator experienced mechanical failure and crashed into the Pacific Ocean.

Of the eleven airmen on board the plane, only Louis and two others survived the crash. The three men were stranded on a raft together in shark infested water for 47 days with no help to be found.

The month and a half at sea proved devastating for these three survivors. It exposed them to the constant sun, air attacks by Japanese bombers, circling sharks, and very little water to drink or food to eat.

To survive, they killed birds that landed on the raft, and collected rainwater. One man died before they finally washed ashore 2,000 miles from their crash site and in Japanese territory. Louis and the plane's pilot, Russell Phillips, survived 47 days stranded in the ocean only to become prisoners of war by their enemies.

After being held captive in a series of prison camps, Louis and Russell were separated and tortured, both psychologically and physically. A camp sergeant, whom prisoners nicknamed The Bird, singled Louis out. The Bird repeatedly abused Louis during fits of psychotic, violent rage. The Japanese likely saved Louis from execution because they saw the former Olympic athlete as a propaganda tool.

He endured captivity for over two years, at which time the U.S. military officially declared him dead. Louis was released from the

Japanese camp after the war ended in 1945, where he returned to the United States.

Traumatized by his torment upon returning home, Louis turned to alcohol, which almost caused him and his wife Cynthia to divorce. What turned Louis away from his alcoholism and began the healing process was hearing a Billy Graham sermon on forgiveness in Los Angeles in 1949.

Eventually, Louis founded a camp for troubled youth called Victory Boys Camp. He also forgave his Japanese tormentors. Some received his forgiveness in person in 1950 when he visited a Tokyo prison where his tormentors were serving their war-crime sentences.

In 1998, Louis returned to Japan to carry the Olympic torch at the Nagano Winter Games. He wanted to forgive his chief tormentor Mutsuhiro "The Bird" Watanabe, but Watanabe refused to meet with Louis and stood by his horrific actions to Louis and the other prisoners.

Louis became a very successful inspirational speaker and evangelist until his death in 2014.

STEP 3

THINK OUTSIDE THE BOX TO UNCOVER OPPORTUNITIES

STEP OUT OF YOUR COMFORT ZONE

It's only after you've stepped outside your comfort zone that
you begin to change, grow, and transform.
—Roy T. Bennett

Growing up as an identical twin, I never had to worry about making friends because I always had my best friend with me. We did everything together until we grew up and got married, my sister first and then me. After we got married, we lived in different cities for a time. As an introvert, I struggled to go to new places and meet new people on my own. I eventually had to learn to dig deep inside myself and pull out my alter ego, Extrovert Laura.

Extrovert Laura is friendly, enjoys getting out and meeting new people, as opposed to Introvert Laura, who is a homebody perfectly content taking Vitamin D tablets.

When I began attending business networking events years ago for my husband's business, my pep talk before walking into the event consisted of me telling myself to go have fun, but if I couldn't find the location, then I could return to the office. However, I had to make a good faith effort. Being geographically challenged, I got lost only twice.

If I found the location, then my next pep talk became, *"Nobody knows you as Introvert Laura, so confidently walk in the room as Extrovert Laura and introduce yourself to the first person you make eye contact."*

The advantage of going to networking events as an undercover introvert is that most of the attendees love to talk about themselves and their business. All I had to do was make the first move to introduce myself and ask them a question such as "Have you come to this event before?" or "What do you do?" I can do this!

After going to additional networking events around town, I recognized people I had previously met, so it became easier to turn into Extrovert Laura and have enjoyable conversations.

* * *

One year after losing our teenage son, my husband encouraged me to go to a happy hour for women entrepreneurs and make new friends. I was hesitant at first since I wouldn't know a soul. I realized Introvert Laura had hidden away Extrovert Laura some time ago. I had to dig deep inside, but I found her.

When I arrived at the restaurant, the hostess showed me to a long table where three women were sitting. We introduced ourselves and had a friendly conversation. As more women arrived, each of the three ladies introduced me to someone new. I was actually enjoying myself instead of looking at my watch thinking of an excuse to leave.

Then I met a gregarious woman, Anne, who passionately told me about an organization where she volunteered her time as a board member, marketing consultant, and mentor. Anne told me how THRU Project bridges the gap between foster care and adulthood for youth who age out of the foster care system. It fascinated me hearing about the successful young people who took part in their programs.

I mentioned to her about going through our adoption process and how we wanted a boy around the age of nine, like our other son. Many families interested in fostering or adopting children were interested in babies or toddlers, which means the odds decrease greatly as children increase in age. This sad statistic continues to break my heart today.

Then my new friend told me of an opportunity to become a mentor with the organization. The youth need a support system to teach them how to make informed decisions and learn basic life skills. I could do that!

I'm so glad I stepped out of my comfort zone by attending that networking event and met Anne who introduced me to THRU Project and their mentorship program.

WHY YOUR COMFORT ZONE IS SO COMFORTABLE

Your comfort zone represents safety and security. It's familiar, so you know what to expect. Even if you are miserable staying comfortable, it's your own comfortable misery.

Stepping out of your comfort zone will cause a slight rise in stress and anxiety because you are facing unknown variables. Some people prefer to stay in their comfortable misery than venture into the unknown. Once you become sick and tired of being sick and tired, you are ready to step out.

That first step might be scary. *What if I try something new and I fail?* This type of question will prevent you from leaving your comfort zone every single time. Instead, look at it from a new perspective.

There is a healthy level of stress that can bring excitement and growth with each new experience. It's about discovering new things about yourself that you didn't realize. You must find that right amount of healthy stress to take that first baby step outside of your comfort zone.

WHAT IF I FAIL? BUT WHAT IF YOU SUCCEED!

Fear can be paralyzing. Fear of heights, fear of snakes, fear of public speaking, fear of the unknown, and especially fear of failure. These are just a few of many fears that hold us back from growth.

In Susan Jeffers' book *Feel The Fear And Do It Anyway*, she breaks fear down into three levels: 1) your exterior situations, 2) your inner state of mind or ego, and 3) the fear that keeps you stuck.

The first level, fear of exterior situations, consists of two types: 1) fears requiring action, and 2) fears about what happens to you. Fears requiring action are making decisions, losing weight, making a mistake, and changing a career. Fears requiring what happens to you include aging, becoming disabled, change, and loss of financial security.

The second level reflects your sense of self and your ability to handle the world. Rejection, success, disapproval, and failure can affect almost every area of your life. As a result, you protect yourself by putting up walls and shutting out the world. This type of behavior becomes destructive.

Jeffers describes level three as "I can't handle it!" meaning at the end of every one of your fears is simply the fear that you can't handle whatever life may bring you. For instance, I can't handle aging (level one) or I can't handle rejection (level two).

THE KEY TO FACING YOUR FEAR

The key to facing your fear is to develop more confidence in your ability to handle obstacles. *Seriously? That's it?*

In a nutshell, yes. Look at your past accomplishments. Did you experience fear at the beginning of them? You most likely did but you pushed through your fear because you accomplished the task. So, keep pushing through your fear!

Why do you have so little trust in yourself? Maybe because your brain is wired to focus on the negative. Some fears are healthy and instinctual, such as being alert to danger. The fears that keep you stuck or hold you back from personal growth are destructive.

It doesn't matter if you know where your self-doubt comes from; you need to start where you are and take the appropriate action to deal with your fears.

WILL MY FEARS EVER GO AWAY?

Short answer? No, but it will get better. The more confidence you gain in your ability to handle your fears, you won't have to work so hard to get rid of them.

The best way to deal with your fear of doing something is to just do it. Pushing through that feeling of fear is less frightening than succumbing to the feeling of continuous misery and hopelessness.

In Todd Herman's book *The Alter Ego Effect*, he discusses how to create your heroic alter ego, like Clark Kent and Superman or Bruce Wayne and Batman. No, you don't have to wear a superhero costume, but you can wear your lucky shirt or a favorite piece of jewelry. I love this concept of creating your heroic alter ego.

Herman tells of one young man who was worried he looked too young for an important job he wanted. He went into the interview wearing a pair of glasses with clear lenses, which gave him more confidence because he felt the glasses made him look older.

Hermann explains that an alter ego can help produce purpose, boost confidence, and generate trust. John Milton, the famous poet, wrote, "The mind is its own place, and in itself can make a heaven of hell, or a hell of heaven."

The power to change dwells inside you. Studies show that using your imagination plugs into the creative area of your brain and fends off negative self-talk, disbelief, and discouragement.

NOTHING TO LOSE, EVERYTHING TO GAIN

If you're trying to feel your fear and do it anyway but feel stuck, ask yourself two questions:

1. What will happen if I don't _____?
2. What will happen if I do _____?

If you've experienced hardship that disrupted your life, what will happen if you don't move on with your life? What will happen if you do move on with your life? Which decision has a better impact going forward?

If your current employer laid off a group of people and may lay off more depending on the economy, *what will happen if you don't look for backup options and are laid off? What will happen if you do look for backup options and are laid off?* Which decision has a better impact on your life?

When your situation is uncertain, don't wait for life to decide your fate. Be proactive. Consider your options and pivot when obstacles come your way. You will learn to say confidently, "I can handle this!" because of your resilient coping skills.

THE SECRET TO GROWTH IS ALL IN YOUR PERSPECTIVE

Fear of failure is the number one reason people don't try. Failure happens when you quit trying. Failure doesn't define you.

So, let's find out the worst thing that can happen if you don't succeed at something. Think of something that you want to try, but you're scared to try. For example, a new hobby, public speaking, a new sport, a new career, a cooking class, a weekend hiking group, etc.

Are you scared of failing at the new activity or embarrassing yourself in front of others? Keep asking yourself why to get to the root of the problem. Why do you lose interest in a new activity when it gets a little difficult? Can you ask someone for help, or do you want someone to do it for you? Why?

Let's look at it from another perspective. What if I succeed? What if I learn a new activity and meet some nice people? What if I make a mistake and learn how to do it a better way? What if I make new friends and start socializing more? What if I volunteer my time and discover that I can make a difference in one person's life or even in a community?

It's not "succeed or fail." It's "succeed or not yet, I'm still learning." There is no failure when you learn. You either learn how not to do something or you learn how to do it better.

Before GPS, I hated driving to new places because I had no sense of direction. Even with GPS, I still get lost (I turn too soon) but I have found so many shortcuts from driving the "scenic routes". I've learned how to get around my city better and I've discovered new restaurants and stores that I never knew existed. See, those weren't failures, they were new adventures.

Life is so much more exciting when you step outside your comfort zone. You have untapped knowledge and talents inside you waiting to get out. Each challenge and risk you experience enlarges your comfort zone. Being open to new experiences also helps you strengthen your resilience and adapt to change.

Step Out of Your Comfort Zone and Succeed

Here are a few simple ways to take baby steps with small risks.

1. **Switch up the easy things in your day.** Drive a different way to work. Style your hair differently. Wake up 15 minutes early and exercise or eat breakfast if you normally don't. Order a

different meal at your favorite restaurant. Video chat instead of texting a friend.

2. **Make a list of why it's beneficial to leave your comfort zone.** Start a list and add to it for a week. It makes me feel like a rebel. I'm taking a small risk because I can. I've always dreamed of playing the violin and now I'm taking lessons! Keep the reasons on your phone or on sticky notes around your house. To get out of your comfort zone, you have to have a good reason to do so.

3. **Start a new story about the new you.** As the motivational speaker, Tony Robbins says, "Divorce our stories, and marry the truth." This can be easier to do if you start a new activity where no one knows you. I don't mean to lie about yourself. In my story above, I turned into Extrovert Laura when I didn't know anyone at networking events. What would the new you do in a new situation? Get a new hairstyle. Update your wardrobe style. Buy new colorful pillows for your beige couch.

4. **Stop procrastinating and do something now.** Don't wait for the perfect time to do something. Do it right now. Throw the clothes hanging on the treadmill onto your bed and walk for 15 minutes. You can do anything for 15 minutes. Set a timer. Clean off the kitchen table. Call and make an appointment you've been putting off. Go through old mail while standing next to the trash can. Sign up for yoga classes you've been talking about for the past year.

Now that you are ready to venture out of your comfort zone, the next chapter will help you overcome challenges and prevent you from retreating to your comfort zone.

THE REST OF MY STORY

Over the past three years, I have had the honor of mentoring a lovely young lady who transformed herself from a troubled youth with a dysfunctional home life to a high school graduate who got accepted into a culinary arts program at a local college. She has a full-time job which enabled her to get her own apartment with the help of the county housing authority. As a youth who aged out of the foster care system, she participates in community programs that are helping her transition into adulthood.

As her mentor, not only am I her loudest cheerleader, but I get to help her learn necessary life skills and utilize local resources to make the transition into adulthood easier. She has made amazing progress. It warms my heart to see her confidence, self-worth, and self-esteem increase with each achievement.

If I had not stepped out of my comfort zone to attend that one business networking event, I would have missed out on an amazing opportunity to work with her.

Exercise: Put It in Action

1. If you want to step out of your comfort zone but cannot take the first step, what are you afraid of? Why?
2. What keeps you inside your comfort zone? Are you happy? Is something missing?
3. What would your life look like if you took a small risk and didn't succeed?
4. What would your life look like if you took the same risk and succeeded?
5. John Milton, the famous poet, wrote, "The mind is its own place, and in itself can make a heaven of hell, or a hell of heaven." What does this statement mean to you? Why?
6. Describe your Alter Ego and its superpowers. What situations would you use your Alter Ego? Why?

THINK OUTSIDE THE BOX

Everyone knew it was impossible until a fool who didn't know came along and did it.—Albert Einstein

In his book *The Survivor Personality*, Siebert tells a story of a Japanese soap manufacturing company that received several complaints from customers who purchased a box of soap, but the box arrived empty.

This prompted an internal investigation, but the engineers could not explain the cause of the problem.

The company saw this as a quality control issue. While management worked on a long-term fix, they told their engineers to come up with a quick solution to prevent empty boxes being shipped out.

The engineers designed an expensive and elaborate scanning system to identify the occasional empty box, but because of its complexity, it would take time to implement. They quickly assembled a prototype to use, but it didn't work correctly, which caused a bigger inconvenience in the production area.

While waiting for the engineer's next move, a line worker came up with a temporary solution of putting a strong fan at the end of the production line. Why? The fan would blow off any empty boxes: a very simple, low-cost, and creative solution unlike the engineer's complex, expensive and detailed one.

THE NINE-DOT CHALLENGE

Creative problem solving doesn't have to be complicated. If you are a parent, you've probably experienced this when trying to keep your young child out of an area or confined to a certain area. No matter how many barricades you put up, a toddler will find a way in.

To test your creative problem-solving skills, try the Nine-Dot Challenge.

Get a pen and some paper and copy the nine dots arranged in a square below. To solve the problem, connect all nine dots using a maximum of four continuous straight lines. You may not lift your pen off the paper or retrace over an existing line. Don't read any further until you've tried to solve the problem.

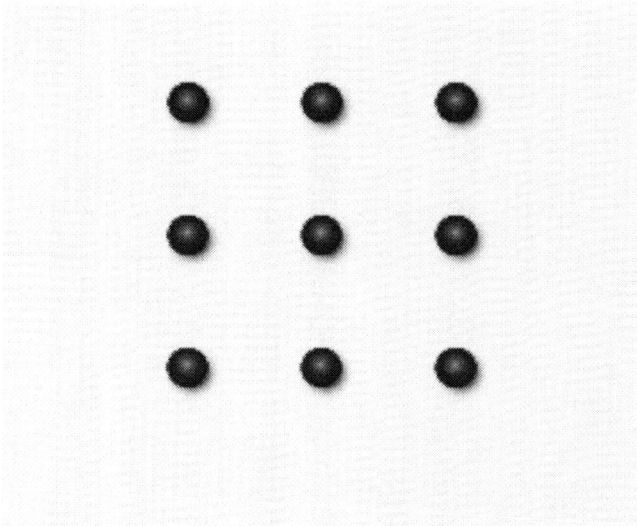

How did you do? If you solved it, give yourself a pat on the back and read on. If you're not there yet, here's a clue to help you. If you're like most people, you may have tried to solve the problem by keeping your lines inside the 'box' created by the dots. But if you look at the instructions, *there is no requirement to do this*. So have another go at solving the problem, allowing yourself to draw outside the box. Again, don't read any further until you've either solved it or given up.

(OK, if you've either solved it or had enough, the solution is on the References page at the end of the book.)

Did it make any difference when I said you could go *outside the box*? Once you think *outside the box*, you open up many more possibilities and it becomes easy to solve the problem. This is true in so many areas of life. Your education, past experiences, and habitual thinking patterns keep you trapped in limiting assumptions.

It takes real effort to challenge these beliefs and be creative. Most of us are very poor at doing this and must work hard at it, unlike creative geniuses to whom this kind of thinking comes naturally.

By eliminating the self-limiting assumption, the solution becomes obvious. In the story earlier, the line worker concluded an empty box is lighter than a filled box, so a strong fan would blow the empty box off the production line.

How many times in business and your personal life do you just try harder with the same assumption? Quite often, thinking about an issue differently makes it much easier to solve.

Creative Problem Solving

I touched on creative problem solving in an earlier chapter using the iCOPE 5-Step Problem Solving Method. It starts with a logical, analytical examination of the root cause of the problem, then pivots to creative solutions.

Finding unusual ideas and solutions that work results from creative thinking, which comes from the same part of the brain that inventors, songwriters, poets, artists, and novelists use to produce their creations. You may not use your creative thinking brain as frequently as they do, but it's available to you to use when you need it.

Constant change requires you to think and act in ways that are new to you, so that your new actions work well. When your new situations are beneficial, then you become more resilient. When you are unable to handle change well, then you are stressed, anxious, and frustrated.

Creative solutions can't be discovered using only logical, analytical problem solving. Creative problem solving begins with the idea that a new, unconventional solution is possible.

Karrie's Story

When Karrie first came to see me, she had a significant problem. She was excited for the opportunity to apply for an open teaching position at an elementary school she'd wanted to teach at for a long time. She'd been out of work and eagerly looked forward to the income. The previous week, however, her doctor diagnosed her with breast cancer and was waiting for one test result to see if a mastectomy was the next step. The test result would be available in three to four weeks.

Karrie's deadline to apply for the teaching position was due in three weeks. She explained to me she really wanted to teach at that elementary school and didn't think she could wait for another position to come available.

I could hear the anxiety in her voice as she expressed concern that her test result would not be available before the application deadline. She wondered if she should apply and hope for the best. Would it look bad if she got the job and had to resign because her test result came back after the deadline showing she needed surgery?

The surgery would require a six to eight-week recovery period at home. If she didn't need surgery, then she would have a minor procedure at the cancer clinic and be out the next day. I could see that Karrie was drowning in "What if's."

During our session together, Karrie realized she was overwhelmed with too many decisions and didn't know what to do. By the end of our session, Karrie concluded she didn't have control over when the test result would be available, but she did have other options to earn income from her hobbies if she couldn't meet the application deadline.

She never considered she could earn income online or in person by teaching people how to paint with watercolors, or repurpose old furniture, or make garden decorations from scrap materials. She was ecstatic that she had other income options. This gave her hope.

Karrie's test result came back a few days after her application deadline, but she had her backup plan in place. She didn't need surgery, but she needed radiation which made her exhausted. She was glad she didn't have to teach while getting her radiation treatments.

Six months later she applied and was accepted to the same elementary school as a substitute teacher. Karrie impressed the principal with her positive outlook and helpful interactions with the children. The principal mentioned to Karrie that she would keep an eye out for any classroom openings.

By implementing the iCOPE Problem Solving Method, Karrie focused on what was in her control and found creative ways to use her superpowers—skills, talents, passions, strengths, and available resources— to uncover opportunities to improve her life.

THE THIRD ALTERNATIVE

In the book, *The 3rd Alternative: Solving Life's Most Difficult Problems* by Stephen R. Covey, he describes how we see most conflicts as having two sides: my way versus your way. My motives are pure; your motives are not. My way is right and just; your way is wrong and maybe unjust. In any case, we see only two alternatives.

Each of these alternatives is deeply set in an established mindset. Each side perceives itself as principled and logical, and the other side as lacking morals and common sense. The deep roots of mindset are attached to our identity and beliefs. So, when you attack my side, you attack me and my beliefs. Conflicts may become frustrating impasses with only two alternatives.

The problem isn't which side you are on, but how you think. The real issue is with your mental paradigm, a model or pattern of thinking that impacts how you behave and which direction to go. The map you see influences what you do, which influences the results you get. If you alter paradigms, then your behavior and outcomes change as well.

When issues arise, we can try "my way or your way," but who is going to concede? Not me and probably not you. Therefore, we can agree to come up with a better solution than combining our two mental maps by looking at a third alternative that we haven't thought of yet. The third alternative is called synergy.

Covey tells the story of his son, David who needed a certain college class to graduate on time but heard the standard line "Sorry, the class is full. You can't get in." He discussed his dilemma with his father who responded "Persist! Come up with a 3rd Alternative." After some discussion, David was prepared to go back and get into that class.

When the registrar's representative said there was no room in that class, David replied he had his own chair to bring, or he'd stand the entire class time. He looked the college staffer in the eye and told her he's going to be in that class regardless because people will drop out. He also added that he was more committed than those who will drop out so he's showing his commitment right now. David got in that class and graduated on time.

Do you understand why it's important to be persistent and find a 3rd Alternative? By creating a win-win solution, all parties are likely to "buy in" and make it happen.

SYNERGY EXPLAINED

Synergy results when one plus one equals ten or one hundred or even one thousand. Synergy happens when two or more people determine together to create a new reality through passion, energy, and ingenuity that exceeds the old reality. It is not a compromise. In a compromise, everyone involved must lose something. Synergy is not resolving conflict but going beyond it to something new and exciting.

Covey gives another example of this concept in his book. A machine that can apply 60,000 pounds per square inch (PSI) on a bar of iron will crush it. A bar of chromium, of the equivalent size, will be crushed at around 70,000 PSI. A bar of nickel will be crushed at around 80,000 PSI. The total PSI of the three bars is 210,000 pounds. Therefore, if all three bars were combined into one bar, it should withstand 210,000 PSI, correct?

No. If all three bars were mixed in certain ratios, the end result of the bar will withstand 300,000 PSI. That's 90,000 pounds of strength that appeared out of nowhere! The metals together are 43 percent stronger than they are individually. That, my friend, is synergy.

When seeking solutions to problems or looking for new opportunities, consider tapping into what you have at your disposal such as your skills, talents, strengths, passion, people, and available resources. How can you use different combinations of your assets to accomplish more instead of using only one?

CRITERIA FOR SUCCESS

To achieve synergy, you need to start with a powerful set of criteria that represents success to all parties involved. If important information is excluded, you will have to start over and rework the solution to achieve true synergy. Successful criteria can take many forms. A blueprint to build a house, a strategic plan to run a business, or a mission statement that sums up your highest aspirations.

Setting successful criteria helps you to better comprehend where you are now so you will be headed in the right direction. Otherwise, you'll start climbing the ladder only to realize later it's leaning against the incorrect wall, and every step will get you closer to the wrong place.

The best environment for finding the 3rd Alternative is where all possibilities are on the table, where everyone can contribute, and no idea is judged. You're not there to debate, critique, or finalize anything; that will come later.

Abundance is the key. Reverse conventional wisdom and turn ideas on their heads. Work fast and set a time limit. You may feel uncomfortable at first, but the more you experiment with the ground rules, the more eager you'll become to see what outcomes arise. If you find yourself struggling to be creative, think like a child. Children are the most synergistic people around.

I remember when my son was a toddler, he'd pull out his favorite toys and excitedly hand me a few green army men and said, "Let's play, Mom!" I didn't remember how to play along and, quite frankly, I felt silly trying to utter creative things to say with my green army men, but my son was having a blast ad-libbing his story lines. I had memories of playing for hours with my Barbies by myself when I was a child. What happened to my creativity?

You know you've arrived at a 3rd Alternative from the thrill of discovery in the air. The childlike excitement of finding hidden treasure. The new alternative takes over and you are in awe of its simplicity, its sophistication, and its success. It embodies the outcome you wanted and enables everyone to win.

SYNERGY IN LIFE

Too many people live a Two-Alternative life. They work or they play. Most people work now in order to play later. With the technological advances made over the years, people continue to work long hours with no goal in mind except to get through the week as quickly and as hassle-free as possible so they can relax on the weekend. Day after day, you get on the hamster wheel, running nowhere. You work hard most of your life to retire at a specific age and enjoy leisure activities for the rest of your days, depending on your health. That's what you've been conditioned to believe. Keep working or retire, and then you'll be happy, and life will be meaningful.

Why not apply the 3rd Alternative to your life now? You can continue going with your life's work well past the "golden age" of sixty-five and still make strong contributions to your family and to the community, responding to the significant needs you see around you. But you don't have to wait until retirement age to enjoy life and even improve your quality of life.

A mission-driven life is exhilarating. Meaningful contributions to society keep your immune system robust and the regenerative parts of the body working. Your meaning and purpose in life can come from new paths you've put off taking.

The more you care, the more you're inclined to take on the large, important issues facing you. This requires the need for more inner strength. The bigger the problem, the more important the issue or relationship, the bigger the need for ample win-win thinking, endurance, tenderness, bravery, appreciation, compassion, perseverance, and creativity. Your success as a 3rd Alternative thinker will come from the inside out.

SURVIVORS HAVE A TALENT FOR SERENDIPITY

Survivors have the ability to turn obstacles into opportunities. Adversity can take your life in a different and better direction than you could have imagined.

Serendipity is not good luck or a lucky accident, it's transforming hardship into growth.

Highly resilient people can turn a life-disruptive event into a gift through creativity. Your ability to turn hardship into growth allows you to discover strengths you didn't know you had.

When looking for the gift from adversity, hunt the good stuff. Ask yourself *"What good can come out of this?"* Look at the situation from all angles. Change is hard but it can lead to new opportunities you would not have pursued if things remained the same.

KEEP YOUR CREATIVITY SHARP

Much like resilience, creativity is a muscle that must be exercised to build strength. It helps you look at objects and situations in new ways. Children excel at this, too. One Christmas, my toddler son was more excited to play with the box than the toy that was packed inside it. If you want to see creativity at its finest, give boxes to young children to play with and watch their imagination run wild.

- **Make a game out of new or different uses for items in your house.** This teaches you to look at items and situations with a different perspective. For example: using an old boot as a planter or building a table out of books.
- **Alphabetize the letters inside words.** Take any word and alphabetize its letters. For example: the word pencil would be spelled C-E-I-N-P. This exercise boosts your brain functions by forcing you to do something unusual with all the information you have. It trains your brain to come up with unforeseen connections and solutions, and to look at problems differently.
- **Solve brain teaser games.** I love Word Search puzzles because I excel at finding hidden words. It's like the letters pop out at me. Other thinking games include Sudoku, Crosswords, riddles, Wordle, and card games. There is a plethora of games to get your creative juices flowing.

The U.S. Airlines pilot "Sully" Sullenberger used his experience and knowledge of glider planes to land his commercial passenger plane on the Hudson River after it struck a large flock of Canadian geese, damaging both engines during liftoff. By imagining landing his glider plane, he was able to save 155 people on board.

Become a self-learner. You don't have to take a class or spend money to expand your knowledge. Read library books, watch YouTube videos, talk to people, volunteer in the community, or learn a new hobby. The more you learn about different topics, the more information you have at your disposal to make certain connections and find new passions.

EXERCISE: PUT IT IN ACTION

1. List the times you came up with a simple solution to a challenging situation. How did that make you feel?
2. Were you able to solve the 9 Dot problem on the first try? Why or why not?
3. How can you apply the 3rd Alternative to a problem you are experiencing?
4. What will you do today to sharpen your creativity skills?

EXPERIENCE POSITIVE GROWTH

Your trauma is not your fault, but your healing is your responsibility.
I am better off healed than I ever was unbroken.—Beth Moore

During my divorce, the idea of starting my life over at age 58 was daunting.

I was married for half my life. Over the past eight years of our marriage, I worked 12–14-hour days, six days a week running my husband's business. How was I going to spend my time now? My son, a grown adult, was responsible, independent, and living a busy life with his fiancé. I did have a handful of close friends, but I hadn't talked to them in quite a while.

I didn't have to like my husband's decision to leave me for another woman or approve of it, but I had to choose whether or not I would accept his decision. If I didn't accept his decision, I would become bitter from reliving the pain and suffering over and over again.

When I saw my two choices, I realized I had to accept his decision and move on. God blessed me with a new heart to start a new life with new opportunities. My counselor asked me, "How are you going to make the most of your new life?"

I became excited about pursuing passions and opportunities I'd had put on hold while dedicating my time to our business. Now I had time to get back to playing the piano. I could find my yarn and fabric and start crocheting and quilting for friends, family, and charities again.

I could finally finish Justin and Grigory's Eagle Scout quilts (made with the limited 2010 "100th anniversary of Boy Scouts" fabric). I also had time to make that memorial quilt with Grigory's favorite t-shirts. I had time to volunteer in the community, read books, and take day trips or weekend trips with my family. I couldn't believe it. I was actually making a bucket list I could check off!

My twin sister Lucy got excited when I told her I was going to bake again. I was known for making homemade bread, scones, cookies, cakes, pies, and muffins. Baking was so therapeutic for me. I could share my goodies with family and friends again. I realized my life wasn't over; it was just beginning. I had choices! I could feel peace, joy, and hope coursing through my veins, and it was a wonderful feeling.

PAIN'S TRANSFORMATIVE POWER

Post-traumatic growth (PGT) is a psychological transformation that can result from the aftermath of a stressful event. It's a way of discovering the purpose of the pain and looking past the struggle you endured. PTG involves life-altering changes that can potentially change the way you observe the world. It comes with a new insight into life, health, money, relationships, and success. PTG is a natural process of healing and growth that can occur in the weeks, months, and years following major life events.

Richard G. Tedeschi and Lawrence Calhoun originated the term "post-traumatic growth" in the mid-90s through their research at the University of North Carolina at Charlotte. Studies show that people who experience PTG flourish in life with a greater appreciation and increased resilience.

PTG goes further than acknowledgement or acceptance. It weaves personal strength and dependence on your own efforts and resources. While the pain may still hurt, you create a new way of redirecting the pain to something useful.

In Tedeschi and Calhoun's research, about 60 percent of people who experienced a wide range of major life events also reported PTG. These major life events included the onset of physical disability, accidents, natural and man-made disasters, combat, rape, sexual abuse, terminal illness, bereavement, divorce, or the onset of a child's serious illness or disability. In the aftermath of such events, many people were able to find some benefit.

Even though PTG provides relief from stressful, major events, growth doesn't make everything better. But it may make it easier to bear the pain when you realize that your suffering was not entirely in vain.

Although growth is natural, it doesn't happen to everyone. In some cases, people who experience no PTG also have experienced little distress following adversity. Their system of core beliefs allows them to comprehend what is happening, and they don't have to rethink what they already know. They can return to their previous way of living with little difficulty. These are the most resilient people. Sometimes these people may have experienced very difficult childhoods growing up. They may have learned the lessons of pain, that life is hard and unfair.

VARIOUS FORMS OF PTG

Different forms of PTG and different combinations can occur within each individual. What it looks like to you may differ from what it looks like to someone else based on what you were like before a major life event, the adversity you experienced, and what you were exposed to afterward.

You may realize that you have already encountered some aspects of growth and recognized positive changes. If you haven't seen any sign of growth yet, then we'll look at various forms so you can recognize it in the future. It's hard to achieve what you cannot imagine.

In their book *The Posttraumatic Growth Workbook*, Richard G. Tedeschi and Bret A. Moore discovered five general types of PTG that people reported:

1. **Personal Strength:** Some survivors of very difficult situations do not think of themselves as special, despite their ability to survive. They might respond to people who admire them, "What was I supposed to do? Give up?" But your strength as a survivor of adversity is something worth recognizing. The daily battle with post-trauma challenges leads you to develop a stronger degree of self-reliance. When it happens to you, you find a way to manage what you're going through by discovering

a strength you had never known or needed before. Just as necessity is the mother of invention, adversity may be the mother of strength. Some parts of what you are going through you must do on your own. No one is going to live your life for you, you must live it. The ability to accept and acknowledge that you can live this new life using your own personal resources can be a source of empowerment and comfort.

2. **Improved Relationships with Others:** While self-reliance is important, so is finding and accepting support. It brings you closer to others. You may find that your relationships become stronger and closer because of learning how compassionate and kind people can be. Growth and strength happen when you know you can rely on others and accept their help. You also gain increased appreciation for people and put forth more effort to deepen your relationships. You realize that there are others who care about you. Not that everyone will respond as you wish in times of need, but most of the time there are some surprises. People whom you may not expect to notice or respond, have been remarkably kind to you.

3. **Appreciation of Life:** One of the most common lessons learned from experiencing loss is that life has much to offer. You are left with a greater appreciation for what you have. You may even realize that your priorities have changed. For survivors of adversity, each simple facet of life may be a magnificent gift. This appreciation of life may show up in gratitude and lead you to slow down and savor each day.

4. **New Life Paths and Possibilities:** Changes in your life path can be as big as a change in careers or as simple as volunteering at a new charitable organization. One outcome you may recognize in yourself is that you cling more strongly to specific beliefs that guide your actions. These beliefs may mirror a new appreciation of life, or your priorities can shift as you appreciate life more. Or maybe you have new goals because your adversity shut the door on old goals. For many people, setting aside what has been important for many years is difficult. You can't expect to switch to a new life path without some struggle and

grief. Out of these losses, something even more significant and useful to you may emerge.

5. **New Understanding of Life's Meaning and Purpose:** As you grapple with what has happened to you, a heightened sense of importance of spiritual matters, or an understanding of how to live life well, may result. Because of your hardship, things about life that once upset you in the past may become trivial now. A new perspective on life may even find you struggling with the major questions about the purpose or meaning of your life. You may think about your religious beliefs, your spiritual sense, or your philosophy of life. The key is to find your own truth about how to live life well.

YOUR NEW LIFE STORY

The stress of adversity presents you with challenges in living but also forces you to consider what your life will look like moving forward. One of the most difficult challenges you must consider is what you believe about the most fundamental aspects of living your life well: what kind of person you are, what kind of world you live in, what makes sense and is meaningful to you, and what your future will be.

What you have gone through (or are still going through) may have been quite extensive and represents a new pathway and new principles. If you understand the logic of what has been happening in your life, these changes you've experienced will be woven into a life story that makes more sense and will be easier to sustain. You will have the insight of knowing that you are making things happen rather than having things just happen to you.

HAPPINESS VS. FULFILLMENT

Psychologists have characterized two types of happiness, both of which trace their beginnings to the ancient Greeks.

- **Hedonic happiness:** The quest for pleasure and the prevention of pain. This is the pleasure you get from eating a snow cone on a hot summer day or the enjoyable things you can do from receiving a large bonus at work. This type of happiness may lead to a lot of enjoyment, but it is often temporary and absent of greater purpose.

- **Eudaimonia:** This kind of happiness is deeper and comparable to seeking personal growth to emerge a better person. This is much closer to the experience of individuals who report PTG. You live life soaked in meaning. You have a certain wisdom seized from experience, and you cherish people you are closest to. You are fulfilled, not simply having a fun time.

Adversity can be transformational. After you bounce back from a major life event and experience positive growth, you will continue to live your life according to the new roadmap laid out for you the day you crossed paths with hardship. You recognize that adversity, for all the agony it brings with it, also presents a remarkable opportunity.

THE REST OF MY STORY

Despite the problems and frustrations surrounding my divorce, I still experienced growth and was able to find joy in my life through gratitude.

Through hardships, I discovered I am a survivor. Through loss, I discovered an appreciation of life. Through closed doors, I discovered new paths that led to new meaning and purpose in life. Through perseverance, I discovered inner strength. Through my positive outlook, I hunted the good stuff and found joy in the little things.

I learned how to transform adversity into a fulfilling life and I'm glad I can share this knowledge with you in this book.

The most important gift I received from my hardships is a stronger faith to trust God and to rely on His plan for me. I am limited in what I can do myself, but God is the God of the Impossible. Through Him, I can do all things, and persevere through each hardship. I have hope and faith that God works all things together for good for those who love Him.

EXERCISE: PUT IT IN ACTION

1. Have you experienced positive growth after adversity? If yes, describe how your life was enriched?
2. Knowing that positive growth happens over time, which of the five forms of growth would you like to see more of in your life?
3. List a few examples in your life that gave you happiness and examples that gave you fulfillment.

CASE STUDY: CORNEL HRISCA-MUNN

*"I play because I love playing drums. I practice and perform because
I want to be taken seriously as a musician, not just observed and casually
admired for my disability. I do what I do because I love it."*
—Cornel Hrisca-Munn

He was born in Romania in 1992 with no forearms and a twisted leg. The hospital staff did not bother making a birth certificate since they did not expect him to live. They took Cornel from his parents, who could not care for his needs, and placed him in an orphanage to die. His parents were too poor to care for him at home but stayed in touch with his whereabouts.

Nine months later, Cornel was still alive. British aid workers Doreen and Ken Munn brought Cornel to the UK to find out what treatment would be best for him. Because of the complexity of his disability, top surgeons decided that amputation of his leg would be the best course of action.

The follow-up care would require Cornel to remain in the UK as there was no provision for artificial limbs in Romania. He would end up returning to the orphanage as before. Cornel's leg was operated on in March 1994.

Three months later, Doreen and Ken Munn adopted Cornel to secure his future medical care. They fit Cornel with his first artificial leg as a toddler. Four weeks later, he was walking unaided.

Cornel was also fitted with an artificial arm but found it too heavy and cumbersome because it restricted his activities. With strong determination, he found he could do better without it. This was the beginning of his many incredible achievements.

In 1995, at the age of three, the Munns took Cornel back to Romania to visit his biological parents. It fascinated them to see his progress.

When he began attending public school, he quickly established himself as competent and as capable as other children his age.

At six years old, Cornel raised 8,500 British pounds by riding his tricycle four miles in a local park. The money raised helped treat a young boy living in Romania who was sick with leukemia. The boy's parents were too poor to pay for the treatments he needed. Cornel's fundraising achievement made the local paper.

In 2003, Cornel, age 11, was awarded the Citizenship Award for his amazing ability of raising funds to help others less fortunate. Later that year, the BBC made a documentary about Cornel, his adoptive family, and his biological family.

In 2004, in recognition of his fundraising efforts, they awarded him the Pride of Britain Child of Courage Award. At his presentation Cornel said he did not want people to pity him and pledged to continue raising money to help others. "I am just like everyone else," he added. "It is just a visual thing and it does not affect my attitude to life. I now plan to try to raise money towards a limb center in Romania."

Later that year, the Limbless Association presented Cornel with the Douglas Bader Award for inspiration to others. Douglas Bader was a Royal Air Force flying ace in World War II whose plane was shot down. After losing both legs, Bader was told he would never fly again, but against all odds he did.

So inspired by Cornel's efforts, in 2005 his school nominated him for the Princess Diana Memorial award for inspiration and success against all odds. The school wrote that the award was in recognition of his outstanding perseverance, his enthusiastic work to raise funds for others facing extreme handicap and hardship, and for overcoming challenges to be successful in school and life.

Soon after, Cornel fulfilled his dream of forming The Cornel Romanian Rehabilitation Centre Trust with his parents to raise funds for a limb center in Romania.

* * *

Cornel discovered his love of playing drums, and a few years later, the bass guitar. In 2007, at age 15, he was one of twelve elite finalists competing for the title of Young Drummer of the Year out of 400 contestants.

He stumbled across the endless world of drum covers on YouTube and, with a grainy webcam, began recording and uploading his own drum covers. In no time, Cornel became a YouTube sensation. Within two weeks of uploading his videos, MTV interviewed him. He appeared on CNN and attracted a lot of social media attention.

A turning point came when he recorded a drum cover of a Foo Fighters song "Everlong", which received over one million views on YouTube. Opportunities came flooding in. He ran drum clinics in the United States and drum festivals across Europe. He even had famous musicians sharing his videos.

Cornel Hrisca-Munn playing drums.
Courtesy of candomusos.com

In early 2018, Cornel performed at a gala in one of Europe's biggest and most distinguished theaters in Barcelona, Spain, in which he played to over 2,500 people in an event that celebrated 25 years of Groups, a Europe-wide organization committed to enhancing the lives of people with disabilities.

Besides receiving his Master of Arts in Philosophy and Theology from the University of Oxford, he is married and continues to play drums and bass guitar professionally with his band. He remains an inspiration to many people today.

Life is a series of trials. Cornel Hrisca-Munn is living proof that it is possible to lead a successful life with the right attitude and mindset, disabled or not.

BONUS

LIVE A LIFE WITHOUT REGRETS

BURN THE SHIPS! NO RETREAT!

The biggest rewards in life are found outside your comfort zone.
Live with it. Fear and risk are prerequisites if you want to enjoy
a life of success and adventure.—Jack Canfield

When I moved from Houston to Pittsburgh, it gave me confidence that I could move to a new environment, make new friends, and develop a new support system. I discovered strengths in me that sat dormant from living too long in my comfort zone back in Texas. Stepping out of it was scary at first, but so rewarding as I discovered exciting adventures in and around Pittsburgh.

After three years living in Pittsburgh, my husband took a job in Washington, D.C., and we moved to Northern Virginia. I loved our little town of Stafford because it was easy to get around, and I experienced all four seasons of weather. What little snow we received melted from the sun, and there were many historical sites all around us to visit.

It was here that I started homeschooling my son Justin in third grade. We joined a very active homeschool group that had an average of forty field trips a month to choose from. We didn't do all of them, but we did stay busy.

One of our memorable field trips was a tour of Ford's Theater in Washington, D.C. which included taking part in a few professional acting lessons on stage before watching the evening performance.

An interesting fact I learned about Ford's Theater was that only Screen Actors Guild (SAG) card holders were allowed on the stage. However, they made an exception for our homeschool group. We received an acting lesson on the stage and it was a thrill of a lifetime! Later that evening, we enjoyed watching the play Shenandoah starring Scott Bakula.

Other homeschool trips included a visit to an Amish community in Lancaster, PA where we toured a dairy farm, enjoyed a delicious homemade lunch, bought handwritten recipe books, and visited an Amish church. We even drove past black horse-drawn carriages traveling the same roads.

Each homeschool trip was filled with history. We toured and participated in a small civil war reenactment at the Civil War Museum in Richmond, VA, and visited many of our founding fathers' homes.

It was also in Virginia that we first learned of the opportunity to adopt Grigory from St. Petersburg, Russia. At the time, I had no idea of all the plans God had in store for us. It took leaving Texas to get the adventure started. I'm so glad God dragged me from Houston to Pittsburgh and then to Virginia, because I experienced amazing adventures I wouldn't have done otherwise.

THE MEANING OF BURN THE SHIPS

The phrase "burn the ships" dates back to 1519 when a Spanish expedition led by Hernán Cortés landed in Mexico. After the long sea journey, he knew his crew was exhausted, but he had to motivate them to explore the new land. Cortés ordered the ships to be burned so his crew would see there was no turning back.

When you choose to leave your comfort zone, difficulties will happen and try to derail you. Feel the fear and use your resilience skills to persevere and overcome any obstacles. Change your perspective to see obstacles and new opportunities. Get excited about new adventures you are about to encounter.

THE THRILL OF THE ROLLERCOASTER RIDE

Remember your younger days at the amusement park and the thrill of standing in line waiting to ride the rollercoaster? You'd grow impatient waiting your turn but also feel a little anxious as you moved forward in line, listening to the screams of excitement from the riders and the roar of the rollercoaster?

Then it's finally your turn to ride the rollercoaster!

How will you behave on this ride? Maybe you were the one who held on tight to the lap bar while screaming with your eyes tightly shut. Or you were the one who embraced the thrill of the ride by keeping your eyes wide open with your hands in the air the whole time. (I was a little of both; I kept my eyes open *while* screaming and holding tightly to the lap bar.)

Either way, you survived the exhilarating ride and most likely decided to ride it again and again, getting braver with each ride. This is what it feels like to keep stepping out of your comfort zone. There's a fine line between anxious and excited. You get to decide where that line is.

GROWING UP AND LOSING OUR "NO FEAR" ATTITUDE

As you get older and learn from your life experiences, it's easy to lose that "no fear" attitude we once had as a child because of our hard knocks along the way. The older you get, you can become risk-averse and find comfort in playing it safe.

Within your comfort zone, you have little incentive to reach new heights of performance. You can go about your routine devoid of risk, causing your progress to plateau.

Your nervous system has a Goldilocks zone of excitement. Too little, and you remain in your comfort zone, where boredom sets in. Too much, and you enter the panic zone, which can stop your progress. Your optimal zone is in the middle where you experience the right amount of excitement and anxiety to step out of your comfort zone into your growth zone.

Having a growth mindset recognizes that not being immediately successful at something can be painful, but it doesn't define you. It becomes a problem to be acknowledged, dealt with, and learned from. If you improve then the setback was not in vain. Failure happens when you give up…so, don't give up.

Instead, reframe your stress from anxiety into excitement, which turns it into positive stress. Society labels stress as bad. Positive stress gives you the energy to push through a public speech, ask someone on a date, and make that tight deadline at work. You choose to label your stress as bad or good, negative or positive, damaging or motivating.

EXPERIENCING THE OBSTACLE COURSE

Once you decide to step out of your comfort zone, you will most likely face obstacles along the way, but that's okay. Nothing worth having comes easy.

Remember those feelings of waiting to ride the rollercoaster, the thrill of the ride, and getting braver with each ride? Well, that's what growth is all about. Instead of calling it "no fear" this time, we'll call it "no regrets."

Think of growth as an ongoing obstacle course. Each time you get past an obstacle, you have more confidence to face the next one. Some obstacles will be easy to move past and others will be harder to overcome, but you'll find a way. Just don't give up. Use your perseverance tools and creative problem-solving skills in your Resilience Toolbox. Obstacles are only steppingstones to opportunities. It's all in your perspective.

BREAK A GOAL INTO SMALLER GOALS TO ENSURE SUCCESS

The best way to ensure success in goal setting is to break down your main goal into smaller, achievable goals. As you complete each smaller goal, you build your self-confidence and your motivation.

When I was young and would complain to my father about facing, in my mind, an insurmountable task, my dad would chuckle and ask me a question, "Laura, how do you eat an elephant?" and I would smile and reply "One bite at a time, Dad."

So here are a few tips on how to eat that elephant:

1. **Write your main goal in specific and measurable terms.**
   Example: Prior to getting married, I didn't finish my last year of college classes. My employer told me I couldn't advance any further without a college degree. My main goal: I want to go

back to college and complete my last year of classes so I can graduate in two years, while continuing to work full time.

2. **Break the main goal into smaller goals with specific and measurable terms.** Example: I have 24 hours of classes to complete in order to graduate in two years which means I can take six hours each fall and spring semester and either take the summer off or take one three-hour class one summer semester if it is available.

3. **Write each smaller goal into specific and measurable terms.** Example: I'll have to finish my work on time so I can make it to class on time. I could ask a co-worker to be my backup when things come up at the last minute. I'll offer to bring them my famous chocolate chip cookies, which they love, as a thank you. I'll have a backup plan to call a friend if I have car trouble on my way to work or class, too.

4. **Evaluate your progress every 4-6 weeks with small rewards for consistency.** If you struggle to stay consistent, then adjust your goals into smaller, doable tasks for success. There is nothing wrong with baby steps if you move forward. A growth mindset realizes it will be tough, but you are prepared to push through the difficult times. Quitting is not an option, if you truly want to reach your goals.

No Retreat on the Road to Success

In this world of instant gratification, it's easy to give up when the going gets tough. You can persevere through challenges by following these six tips to succeed and not retreat:

1. **Remember Why You Started** – Remind yourself of the goal you want to achieve and why. If you want to lose weight, put a picture up of you at a previous weight on the refrigerator with the question "Am I hungry or bored?" or tape that picture onto your gym bag. It's easy to make excuses to quit or put it off, but it's harder to stay motivated. Take baby steps. Consistency

will reap rewards. Excuses will reap consequences. Which one do you choose?

2. **Identify Why You're Considering Giving Up** – If you make excuses to quit or procrastinate, ask yourself why? Are your goals or expectations set too high? Do you need to lower your expectations or break down your goal into smaller goals to succeed? Baby steps will still keep you moving forward and are better than giving up. Adapt and overcome. Remember the saying "How do you eat an elephant? One bite at a time."

3. **Visualize Your Ultimate Result** – Some people make a visualization board with inspiring pictures and words to help them stay motivated to reach their goal. Find an easy way to track your progress with short-term goals. You'll gain confidence along the way and will stay motivated to reach your goal.

4. **Find Support and Encouragement** – You can receive encouragement from family and friends or join a social media group. It also gives you the opportunity to help others by sharing tips and resources that helped you on your journey. Your story of perseverance can be someone else's survival guide.

5. **Celebrate Small Wins** – It is very important to celebrate small wins. Our brain is wired to give up at the smallest setback. However, a setback is not final if you learn from it, then it becomes a teachable moment or a lesson learned. As Thomas Edison said, "I never view mistakes as failures. They are simply opportunities to find out what doesn't work."

6. **Find the positive every day** – Hunt the good stuff and be grateful for each step forward. Your progress might not be going as fast as you expected but be grateful that you are still moving forward. You came this far without giving up and you can do it one more day. Keep your eye focused on today's goal when it gets tough. Go back to the beginning of your journey so you can see how far you've come in reaching your goal.

It takes courage to step out of your comfort zone into your growth zone. The key to success is to think of what could go wrong along the way and be proactive, not reactive. You are resilient. You are a survivor. You have skills, talents, strengths, character, and human resources to tap into. Use them all to get around any obstacles in your path.

EXERCISE: PUT IT IN ACTION

1. List 1 to 3 goals you want to achieve and your action steps to achieve them. Are they too big? Do you need to break them into smaller goals?
2. Make a plan of action to deal with setbacks when you step out of your comfort zone. Think of any obstacles that can keep you from reaching your goal and what you will do to overcome them.
3. Which of the six tips of The Road to Success are most beneficial to you? Why?

LIVE YOUR BUCKET LIST NOW

Twenty years from now you will be more disappointed by the things you didn't do than by the ones you did do. So throw off the bowlines, sail away from the safe harbor. Catch the trade winds in your sails. Explore. Dream. Discover.—Mark Twain

Oscar Wilde once said, "To live is the rarest thing in the world. Most people exist, that is all." Some of us may wonder if there is even a difference between "to live" and "to exist".

Both words are verbs and mean to remain alive. However, we often use them in contrasting contexts. Existing means to do what is necessary to stay alive. Living means to enjoy life and savor every moment. This is the key difference between existing and living.

There was a time in my life that I only existed. I was busy with my husband's business, caring for my family, and dealing with my health problems. I got up every morning and did the same thing: my duty. Self-care involved soothing myself with comfort food while sitting at the computer. I had to look at my phone to know what day it was since I worked seven days a week. I remember thinking, *"Is this as good as it gets?"* I was existing in life, and I was miserable.

TOP FIVE REGRETS OF THE DYING

An Australian nurse, Bronnie Ware, spent many years working in palliative care, accommodating her patients in the last 12 weeks of their lives. She wrote about their dying epiphanies in a blog that gathered so much attention that she put her information into a book called *The Top Five Regrets of the Dying.*

#1. I wish I'd had the courage to live a life true to myself, not the life others expected of me.

Bronnie wrote that this was the most common regret of all. When people realize that their life is almost over and look back clearly on it, they see how many dreams went unfulfilled. Most people had not achieved half of their dreams and had to die knowing that it was because of choices they made or had not made. Health brings freedom very few understand until they no longer have it.

#2. I wish I hadn't worked so hard.

This was a deep regret for every male patient she nursed. They missed their children's youth and their spouse's companionship. Women spoke of this regret as well, but because most were from an older generation, many of the female patients were not the breadwinners.

#3. I wish I'd had the courage to express my feelings.

Many patients said they suppressed their feelings to keep the peace with others. As a result, they settled for an ordinary existence and never reached their full potential. As a result, many gained illnesses relating to the bitterness and resentment they lugged around with them.

#4. I wish I had stayed in touch with my friends.

They had not truly realized the rich gift of old friends until their dying weeks, and it wasn't always possible to find them to express their gratitude. Many had become so caught up in their own lives that they had let precious friendships drift away over the years. They felt deep regret about not giving friendships the time and effort that they deserved. Everyone misses dear friends when they are dying.

#5. I wish I had let myself be happier.

Many did not comprehend until the end of their life that happiness is a choice. They had remained stuck in old patterns and habits. Their comfort zone spilled over into their emotions as well as their physical lives. Fear of change made them pretend to others, and to themselves, that they were satisfied with their life, when deep inside they desired to laugh joyously and have silliness in their life again.

* * *

You are continually learning and developing. Each new experience influences how you look at the world and the choices you make. You may choose not to do something at age 25 and then decide to do it at age 40—after your life experiences provide new context and insight.

Throughout your life, it's important to step back repeatedly and ensure that you're living the life you want in order to minimize your end-of-life regrets. To get you started on your own assessment, here is a list of common regrets.

Most Common Regrets in Life

- Not doing more for others
- Not nurturing good relationships
- Not ending abusive relationships sooner
- Not asking that person out
- Letting the passion die in romantic relationships
- Being an inattentive partner
- Getting divorced too soon
- Staying married for their kids
- Holding on to grudges
- Not preparing their kids for independence
- Not spending more time with their kids
- Spending too little time with their parents
- Not finding fulfillment
- Being too tough on themselves
- Not seeking counseling sooner
- Quitting school
- Not accomplishing more
- Not trying to land that dream job
- Working too much
- Not taking vacations
- Not traveling more

- Not being more adventurous
- Not being more spontaneous
- Not eating healthier
- Not doing more to maintain their well being
- Letting friendships fizzle out
- Missing out on the little moments
- Not getting to know people better
- Not apologizing more
- Being ungrateful
- Worrying about other people's opinions
- Not standing up for others
- Not standing up for themselves
- Setting aside their passions
- Muting their real personality
- Ignoring their instincts
- Taking life too seriously
- Prioritizing practicality over fun
- Being unkind
- Not being more present
- Spending too much time worrying
- Not seeing someone before they died
- Not leaving a legacy

Don't let missed opportunities turn into a life of regrets.

CREATE YOUR BUCKET LIST

Whether it's visiting an active volcano, skydiving out of an airplane, or seeing new places of interest with your family or friends, you most likely have things you'd like to achieve during your lifetime. Making a bucket list can help you prioritize your hopes and dreams, and to stay focused on making them a reality. The best time to get started is now, because there really is no time like the present!

Creating your bucket list shouldn't be a quick, five-minute activity where you scribble a few ideas on a scrap of paper or in your phone. If you're going to strive to realize your dreams, then you need to put some thought into the process.

NAME IT

Whatever title you choose, it should remind you that your list contains some of your most important goals and your greatest desires. Your bucket list isn't about dreaming amazing things; it's about *accomplishing* amazing things.

CHOOSE THE LENGTH

I do not mean this to limit your dreams but to make your first bucket list more manageable, both in creating it and achieving what you write down. By keeping to a shorter list initially, it becomes easier to focus on achieving your goals. Fifteen items look much more manageable than 150. You can always add items later after you check some off.

BREAK IT DOWN

Create your list in bite-sized chunks or categories. For example, you can assign one list to travel destinations in or out of the country, another to adventures, another to doing things with family or friends, and one for home goals.

You could also create a list of smaller, more immediately achievable goals, such as dining at an award-winning restaurant or attending a local festival. Keep a separate list of goals that would take a longer time to achieve, such as learning to fly a small plane or playing a difficult instrument. Other lists you can create could be for goals to achieve before reaching a certain age, or for a specific season, such as a summer or fall bucket list.

DISCOVER IDEAS

The simplest way to uncover ideas for your bucket list is to envision the things you've always wanted to do. If you have wanted to stay overnight in a 12th century Scottish castle, enroll in a pastry class, visit all the national parks, or spend a week at an all-inclusive resort in Belize, then write it down.

Remember, you're still in dreaming mode, so there is no dream too big or too small! Expand this list by using your friends' and family's bucket list ideas as inspiration. If you still need more ideas, peruse websites and magazines, or talk to a travel agent.

TAKE TIME FOR SELF-REFLECTION

Remember, your bucket list is unique to you and means that self-reflection is a priority. Interviewing yourself is a wonderful way to find inspiration. Ask yourself the following questions and write down your answers.

- What are your favorite regional cuisines?
- Are there any artistic activities or sports you've wanted to try?
- What personal adventure stories do you dream of sharing with your children or grandchildren?
- What experiences have you dreamed of sharing with your spouse or best friend?
- If you had one month left to live, what would you do?
- If you could travel anywhere in the world, where would you go?
- What cultures or cultural traditions fascinate you?

START REVIEWING YOUR LIST

When you're done thinking of ideas and writing them down, it's time to turn your ideas into a reality. The purpose of creating your bucket list is to help you concentrate on living life to the fullest. It's ensuring that you won't have regrets in your golden years about not doing the things you really wanted to.

Whether your items are well-balanced and cover all your interests or they're centered on luxury experiences, adventure travel, or foodie experiences, they're meant to inspire you. Your bucket list will always be a work in progress. Keep it handy and refer to it frequently—it will motivate you to stay focused on the things that really matter!

NINE TIPS TO LIVE A LIFE WITHOUT REGRETS

Are you living a no-regrets life? You don't have to wait until you're an empty nester or retired. You can start right now with these top ways to live a fulfilling life.

1. **Take ownership of your life.** Are you living your aspirational dreams or are you living the life someone else set for you? If you have to suffer the consequences of your own actions, then you should be the one in charge of your decisions. Pay attention to what you feel in your heart you are called to do in life and do it. Don't worry about what others think you should do.

2. **Close the door to prior regrets.** Life is too short to live with coulda, shoulda, and woulda regrets. There are some previous regrets we must accept and move on. The important thing is to get out there and try again because there may be something better. Example: I may not get back into playing tennis, but my sister and I could play as partners in pickleball.

3. **Feel that fear and do it anyway.** What if you get to the end of your life and wish you didn't have so many regrets from your fear of failure? We all know that feeling right before making a decision of "What if?" It's okay to feel that feeling but do it anyway. So, what if we fail? If we learned something, then it

becomes a lesson, not a failure. Example: What if I look funny learning to play pickleball? I'll get the hang of it the more I play, and I can ask other players I meet for friendly advice. What do I have to lose?

4. **Don't hide your feelings.** Is there someone you need to tell, "I'm sorry" or "Thank you" or "I love you"? Our days are numbered here on earth, so don't wait to share your feelings with someone. They might have been waiting a long time to hear you say those special words.

5. **Take risks.** Step out of your comfort zone and experience new things. You don't have to take giant steps. Baby steps are just fine, and you can take one or two each day. By stepping out of your comfort zone, you'll achieve a more fulfilling and successful life.

6. **Find humor in life.** Life is too short to spend time taking everything so seriously, especially things beyond your control. Finding humor in everyday life will increase your overall health. The key to having a more enjoyable life is to find good in every situation and find reasons to laugh, even at yourself. Laughing is a great stress reducer.

7. **Practice kindness.** A smile or a kind gesture can make someone's day brighter. Being kind is an easy way to enhance our lives and others, whether we know them or not. Volunteering in your community is a wonderful way to show kindness to others.

8. **Be authentic.** Our uniqueness makes us who we are. Our beliefs, core values, personality traits, strengths, and weaknesses prepare us for our purpose in life. By being authentic, we give others permission to do the same.

9. **Live in the present.** The past is the past, and the future is uncertain. The present is a gift, so treasure the moment. As we get older, time seems to fly by. I remember as a child, I thought time moved too slowly. But now that I'm older, the weeks pass so quickly. Make the most of each day and enjoy each moment. Before you go to bed, list three to five things you are grateful for that happened during your day. And do it

again the next day, and the next. You will find more joy in your life as you continue to practice gratitude.

FLOURISHING

Flourishing moves beyond the boundaries of simple happiness or wellbeing; it embodies a wide range of positive psychological factors and offers a more holistic view of what it means to feel well and happy.

According to the "founding father" of positive psychology, Dr. Martin Seligman, flourishing, or well-being theory, results from uncoerced choice: what free individuals will choose for their own sake.

Seligman developed the PERMA model to explain what contributes to a sense of flourishing. PERMA can be measurable and teachable.

The five elements in this model are:

1. **P**ositive emotions: The positive emotions or pleasures you experience in the moment; warmth, comfort, rapture, ecstasy, fun, etc.
2. **E**ngagement: Flow happens when your highest strengths are perfectly matched with the challenges that come your way. You may become absorbed in an activity that gives you the feeling of time stopping, often referred to as flow.
3. **R**elationships: You most likely shared your highest points in life with other people around you, whether it was with a few close friends, family, or a large group.
4. **M**eaning: Meaning and purpose in life is enriched from belonging to and serving something bigger than yourself.
5. **A**ccomplishments: Achieving your goals through self-discipline and resilience.

Using this model as your framework, flourishing is what you experience when you increase your positive emotions, engage with your work or hobbies, develop deep and meaningful relationships, find meaning and purpose in life, and achieve your goals through cultivating and applying your strengths and talents.

To find out your PERMA score, you can visit Dr. Seligman's Authentic Happiness website at *www.authentichappiness.org* to take a free assessment.

Another handy questionnaire for measuring flourishing comes from well-being expert Ed Diener. The Flourishing Scale is a brief 8-item summary measuring your self-perceived success in important areas such as relationships, self-esteem, purpose, and optimism. The scale provides a single psychological well-being score. It is not based solely on Dr. Seligman's PERMA model, but it has overlapping elements.

The Flourishing Scale, as Diener and colleagues named it, is rated on a scale from 1 (strongly disagree) to 7 (strongly agree):

1. I lead a purposeful and meaningful life.
2. My social relationships are supportive and rewarding.
3. I am engaged and interested in my daily activities.
4. I actively contribute to the happiness and well-being of others.
5. I am competent and capable of the activities that are important to me.
6. I am a good person and live a good life.
7. I am optimistic about my future.
8. People respect me.

The responses are scored by adding up each value for a total score from 8 (lowest possible flourishing) to 56 (highest possible flourishing).

IMPROVE YOUR CHANCES OF FLOURISHING

None of these steps to flourish are easy, but the outcome is worth it. When you enjoy deep and gratifying relationships, engage your days with positive experiences, have fun, and seek fulfillment in your pursuits, you have more meaning and purpose in your life.

Here are a few more suggestions:

- **Commit to experiencing the good things in life.** Plan fun, exciting, meaningful, and fulfilling events regularly. Set a variety of small goals for reaching milestones in life that are important to you and savor the event when you achieve those milestones.

- **Focus on having more fun.** Schedule simple activities to enjoy life's pleasures more than you currently do. Plan a short vacation, go out for a nice meal, or book a fun event you've always wished to try. Come up with ideas to smile more, laugh more, and enjoy yourself more or with other people.
- **Improve your sense of purpose and meaning in life.** Establish what values you cherish most and focus on these as you work, learn, love, and live. Ensure you are living a life that is true to your values.

It is possible to transform pain into a new purpose and live a life with no regrets. The iCope2Hope Resilience Framework is your tool to develop a growth mindset, overcome challenges, and uncover opportunities to flourish in life.

EXERCISE: PUT IT IN ACTION

1. As you reflect on your life, list any regrets you have and why.
2. Do you have a bucket list? If yes, are you checking items off?
3. If you don't have a bucket list, start one. Will you have one or more lists? Answer the bucket list questions within this chapter.
4. Of the nine ways to live a no-regrets life, which ones do you struggle with?
5. Go to *www.authentichappiness.org* and take the PERMA assessment. What areas do you need to improve your score?
6. Instead of going to the Authentic Happiness website, answer the eight questions in the Flourishing Scale above. What areas do you need to improve your score?
7. How can you improve your chances of flourishing?

LEAVE A LEGACY OF RESILIENCE

All good men and women must take responsibility to create legacies that
will take the next generation to a level we could only imagine.
—Jim Rohn

A legacy is anything handed down from the past, as from an ancestor or predecessor.

A legacy is significant because it's thought to be the key to the ongoing bedrock of life. When a person passes on, the only thing friends and family have is what that person left behind.

It does not need to be a great contribution that affects society. It may be a trinket, a tradition, an idea shared by a community, a home that is cherished. It can also be continuing the family line, such as with grandchildren and great grandchildren.

Everyone has a responsibility to leave behind a legacy.

This is an act of benevolence. A person should contemplate the future without them, rather than themselves in the present. Building a legacy and leaving an impression bolsters the larger picture, which impacts individuals, families, and entire communities down the line.

WHY RESILIENCE?

No parent wishes for any adversity to strike their child, but in reality, you must expect challenges and guide your children to prepare for them. Change is inevitable, growth is optional.

In *Building Resilience in Children and Teens*, Dr. Kenneth Ginsburg discusses why you can't raise completely invulnerable children. Your goal must be to raise kids who are capable of handling the bumps and bruises that the world disperses.

You need to encourage them to cope with adversity by bouncing back from setbacks. Help them find joy in small things when they are having a bad day. You want them to establish resilience skills now in order to overcome challenges in the future.

Resilience is the ability to rise above difficult circumstances while moving forward with confidence and optimism. Resilience is a growth mindset that sees challenges as opportunities for a better life.

It's not that you want your children or grandchildren to seek problems, but you understand that setbacks will strengthen them. You wish for them to seek creative ways to solve problems that are within their control instead of engaging in self-doubt, negative thinking, or even victimization.

Resilience is the trait parents want to see in their children and grandchildren so they can navigate a stressful, perplexed world while enjoying its bountiful pleasures. Children who learn to be flexible are more successful because they stretch their limits and learn from their mistakes. Resilience and a growth mindset may be a primary factor in deciding not only who will adapt, but who will flourish.

All children are born with innate resilience. Some children seem inherently equipped with an ability to bounce back faster from obstacles, while others require extra support. Regardless, all children can become more resilient.

You recognize how stressful your life is. Families are continuously rushing around. Kids' schedules are overbooked with academic and extracurricular activities. Peer pressure causes them to take bigger risks. Parents, teachers, and coaches pressure them to improve their performance.

Social media tells them they aren't cool enough, thin enough, fashionable enough, or attractive enough. It's important for children to tap into their inner strengths, persevere and overcome difficult challenges, and be ready for future obstacles.

Children can't do it completely on their own. Parents need to take the lead in building their resilience, but the community of adults that encircle them also influences a child's capacity to flourish. When children are recognized for their strengths and encouraged to reach their potential, they become self-motivated to overcome their challenges.

SHARE THE ICOPE2HOPE RESILIENCE PROCESS

You have in your hands what you need to leave a legacy of resilience to your children, grandchildren, or youth that you work with. You can teach them the iCope2Hope Resilience Process.

1. *Develop a Growth Mindset*: Practice radical acceptance with the Serenity Prayer; conquer change by facing your fear and stretching yourself; and use the three things always in your control—thoughts, words, actions.
2. *Discover Your Superpowers:* Learn how to bend and not break with resilience; identify your skills, talents, passions, character strengths and available resources; implement the iCOPE 5-Step Problem Solving Method.
3. *Uncover Opportunities:* Step out of your comfort zone and live a life without regrets; think outside-the-box to solve problems and uncover opportunities to experience positive growth.

Children need to realize they can change what's in their control and influence what happens to them. It's also important that they acknowledge when they do not have control so they can radically accept it. They always have choices to change their life for the better.

Leaving a legacy of resilience prepares the next generation to overcome challenges and live a fulfilling life. What a wonderful gift to receive!

ACKNOWLEDGEMENTS

Writing this book was much harder than I thought and more rewarding than I could have ever imagined.

None of this would be possible without my business coaches and mentors, Jonathan Milligan and Marisa Shadrick. The good Lord brought Jonathan and his team into my life at just the right time when I had to start over at age 58. Words cannot express the gratitude I have for Jonathan and Charity Milligan, Jodie Vee, Val Brown, Cory Peppler, Lynn Friesth, Roxanne Oates, and Bryan Buckley. A special thanks to Cory Peppler for his patience, humor, and expertise while editing my book. All of you made it possible for me to get my message of hope out to those struggling to move on after adversity.

A special thanks to my amazing son and daughter-in-love, Justin and Abbie Broome, (and my future grandchildren) who cause my heart to overflow with joy when I am around them. I am blessed beyond words that God chose me to be your mother.

To the Mangum family, who provide endless love, laughter, and funny stories each time we gather throughout the year. Specifically, my Giggle Twin (and identical twin), Lucy Mangum Dio, and her daughter Evie and son Austin; our younger brother Larry Mangum and his wife Vicki, their son, Zachary Mangum and his wife Bethany and their daughter Amelia, and younger son Jared Mangum.

To our parents in Heaven, Lewis and LaVerne Mangum, who were wonderful role models and taught us the importance of family values. To our family friend Linda Yeager, who taught us how to play Rummikubs at our family gatherings and gives "friendly competition" a new meaning.

To "Uncle' Bob Hyde, who keeps the Luv Ya Blue and Luv Ya Lew memories alive.

To Kary Oberbrunner and his Igniting Souls team. Thank you for the opportunity to take part in the Author Academy Elite program.

Finally, to all the extraordinary people in this world who overcame hardship and share their inspiring stories publicly so that the gift of resilience continues to give others hope.

REFERENCES

BIBLIOGRAPHY

Britt, B. A., and W. Kalow. "Malignant hyperthermia: a statistical review." Canadian Anaesthetists' Society Journal 17.4 (1970): 293-315.

Burpo, Todd, and Lynn Vincent. Heaven Is for Real: A Little Boy's Astounding Story of His Trip to Heaven and Back. Thomas Nelson Publishers, 2010.

Calhoun, Lawrence G., and Richard G. Tedeschi, eds. Handbook of posttraumatic growth: Research and Practice. Routledge, 2014.

Collins, Tyler. "The Complete History of the Serenity Prayer." Lighthouse Treatment Center, 4 Mar. 2021, https://lighthousetreatment.com/the-complete-history-of-the-serenity-prayer/.

Covey, Stephen R. The 3rd Alternative: Solving Life's Most Difficult Problems. Free Press, 2011.

Diener, Ed, et al. "New measures of well-being: Flourishing and positive and negative feelings." Social Indicators Research, vol. 39, 2009, pp. 247-266.

Ginsburg, Kenneth, R., with Martha M. Jablow. Building Resilience in Children and Teens. American Academy of Pediatrics, 2015.

Hamilton, Scott. Finish First, Winning Changes Everything. Thomas Nelson Publishing, 2018.

---. "Make It Count: Scott Hamilton Discusses His Cancer Journey." Cure Today, 6 June 2020, www.curetoday.com/view/

make-it-count-scott-hamilton-discusses-his-cancer-journey. Accessed 12 Nov 2022.

Herman, Todd. The Alter Ego Effect. HarperCollins Publishers Inc., 2019.

Hillenbrand, Laura. Unbroken: A World War II Story of Survival, Resilience, and Redemption. Random House, 2010.

Hrisca-Munn, Cornel. "My name is Cornel, and I'm a drum-a-holic—My Story." Cornel Sticks-for-Hands. 22 Aug 2018, https://thecorneltrust. wordpress.com/cornels-story. Accessed 12 Nov 2022.

Jeffers, Susan. Feel The Fear and Do It Anyway. Ballantine Books, 2006.

Kubler-Ross, Elisabeth, and David Kessler. On Grief and Grieving: Finding the Meaning of Grief Through the Five Stages of Loss. Scribner, 2014.

Niemiec, Ryan M., and Robert E. McGrath. The Power of Character Strengths. VIA Institute on Character, 2019.

Ch. 10 Think Outside the Box–Solution to Nine-Dot Challenge

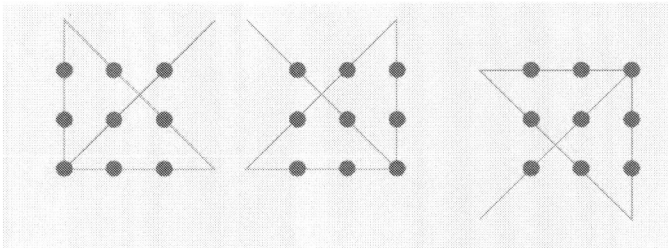

ABOUT THE AUTHOR

Laura Mangum Broome is a Resilience Coach and the founder of iCope2Hope. She teaches people who struggle to move beyond adversity how to transform pain into purpose so they can thrive in life. She developed her 3-Step Resilience Framework after experiencing her own hardships including breast cancer, losing her teenage son to suicide, serious health issues resulting in her heart transplant at the beginning of COVID-19, and one-month later, a sudden divorce after 27 years of marriage. By learning how to overcome her adversities, she is a victor and wants to share this knowledge with others. Laura enjoys mentoring youth in foster care, playing the piano, laughing, and spending time with her family. She lives a joyful life in South Texas. To learn more, visit www.iCope2Hope.com.

Also By Laura Mangum Broome
Fiercely Faithful: Be Inspired, Find True Purpose, and Live a Miraculous Life
Compiled by Dr. Elizabeth Clamon
Laura's Chapter: God's Plan for Growth After Adversity

WHAT'S NEXT?

LEARN HOW TO
FLOURISH AFTER ADVERSITY

Access Laura's FREE Resilient Resources at:

https://www.icope2hope.com/resources

Learn the latest tools, tips, and strategies on how to
move beyond adversity so you can
discover new opportunities to flourish in life.

Made in United States
Troutdale, OR
12/05/2023